BOLD FLAVORED VEGAN COOKING

Healthy Plant-Based Recipes with a KICK

CELINE STEEN

Author of *The Complete Guide to Vegan Food Substitutions*

PAGE STREET
PUBLISHING CO.

PAGE STREET
PUBLISHING CO.

First published in 2017 by

Page Street Publishing Co.

27 Congress Street, Suite 105

Salem, MA 01970

www.pagestreetpublishing.com

Distributed by Macmillan, sales in Canada by The Canadian Manda Group.

21 20 19 18 17   1 2 3 4 5

ISBN-13: 978-1-62414-390-8

ISBN-10: 1-62414-390-3

Library of Congress Control Number: 2016960303

Cover and book design by Page Street Publishing Co.

Photography by Celine Steen

Printed and bound in China

As a member of 1% for the Planet, Page Street Publishing protects our planet by donating to nonprofits like The Trustees, which focuses on local land conservation. Learn more at onepercentfortheplanet.org.

FOR THE ANIMALS, ALWAYS.

INTRODUCTION

Believe it or not, there are worse things for a hardworking cook to hear than "The stove's not working and our dinner party starts in 30 minutes!" or "The refrigerator went kaput during our weekend getaway and all the food is ruined." The most dreaded words may very well be "Will someone please pass the salt?" uttered when the meal you've spent hours preparing turns out to be extremely bland and boring, letting everyone down including the dog. Especially the dog.

We've all been there. You prepare a meal with the best intentions, with or without recipes at hand, and everything you were hoping for doesn't turn out at all the way you planned.

I adopted a vegan lifestyle more than a decade ago, and veganism has become more popular than ever over the years. Yet, despite all the brilliant vegan cooking literature out there, some people still assume that it's a boring, bland diet we inflict upon ourselves. One that involves steamed, unseasoned tofu with boiled broccoli topped with sprouts. If only they knew . . . and now they can!

Creating big, bold, exciting flavors for vegan and vegan-friendly cooks is what this book is all about. With the myriad of spices, umami-rich ingredients and clever cooking techniques that are all within our reach, there is no reason for anyone to ever eat a boring dinner again.

Celine Steen

RECIPE ICONS

Many of the recipes you'll come across in this cookbook are labeled with one or more of the following icons:

Gluten-Free: Recipes that have the potential to be free of gluten, provided you check ingredients for safe use and purchase ingredients that are certified gluten-free. Contact the manufacturer directly for the most current information.

Soy-Free: Recipes that have the potential to be free of soy-based products. Check labels and get in touch with the manufacturer for the most current information. Keep in mind soy can be found in unexpected foods, such as nut milks, vegetable broth, chocolate and cooking sprays.

Oil-Free: Recipes that are made without the use of extracted oils. Note that these recipes will not necessarily be low-fat as they may contain foods that are rich in natural fats, such as nuts and avocados.

In A Hurry: Recipes that take less than 30 minutes to prepare, provided you have intermediate cooking or baking skills.

Chapter One

SAVORY

This is a whole chapter dedicated to the wonders created by umami-rich ingredients. Think of dried shiitake mushrooms, sun-dried tomatoes, double-concentrated tomato paste, matcha green tea, miso, nutritional yeast, tamari and the list goes on. The umami taste is a surefire way to bring a meaty-like quality to the vegan foods we eat, without having to compromise our ethics.

Umami, also known as the fifth taste, works its delicious magic in the following recipes to create dishes with well-rounded flavors. It helps demonstrate once again that there's nothing to be missed when following—and enjoying!—a vegan lifestyle.

For more information about the most umami-rich, cruelty-free ingredients, please refer to page 199. And be sure to incorporate them in your everyday cooking experiments. Time to get this savory show on the road!

PULLED JACKFRUIT ROLLS

I love how sneaky developing some recipes can be; you never know for certain how they will turn out. Then they go and far exceed your expectations when you have that first bite. The jackfruit is even better when prepared ahead of time, so feel free to make it the day before for quick sandwiches the next day. And don't skip the Asian Pear Pickles (page 193). This is a sum-of-all-its-parts kind of sandwich, and the pickles definitely seal the deal.

YIELD: 8 sandwiches

1 tbsp (15 ml) grapeseed oil or olive oil

1 bell pepper (any color), trimmed, cored and chopped

4 large cloves garlic, peeled and minced

1 medium red onion, trimmed, peeled and chopped

2 (20-oz [567-g]) cans young green jackfruit in brine, drained and rinsed

1/2 cup (160 g) Gochujang Paste (page 180) or store-bought

1/3 cup (90 g) organic ketchup

1 1/2 tbsp (30 g) agave nectar

3 tbsp (45 ml) fresh lime juice

1 1/2 tbsp (23 ml) reduced-sodium tamari

2 tbsp (30 ml) Mushroom Dashi (page 181)

1/2 tsp Lapsang Souchong tea leaves (or 1/4–1/2 tsp liquid smoke, to taste)

2 tsp (8 g) Pickled Ginger (page 175), minced

8 vegan french bread rolls, lightly toasted

Regular flavor Faba-lous Mayo (page 167) or store-bought

Garnishes: Shredded red cabbage, sliced English cucumber, sliced scallions, Asian Pear Pickles (page 193), lime wedges

Place the oil, bell pepper, garlic and onion in a large pot. Heat on medium-high and cook for 4 minutes, just to start releasing the flavors and to soften slightly. Add the jackfruit, stirring to combine, and cook for another 2 minutes.

In the meantime, whisk the gochujang paste, ketchup, agave, lime juice, tamari, dashi and tea in a medium bowl. Pour onto the vegetables along with the ginger. Bring to a low boil, stirring to combine. Reduce the heat to a simmer, cover and cook for 1 hour, stirring occasionally and adjusting the heat as needed. Use a potato masher or 2 forks to shred the jackfruit; be careful so as not to scrape and damage the bottom of your pot.

If preparing the day before, let the jackfruit mixture cool completely before storing in an airtight container in the refrigerator. Slowly reheat in a pan on medium heat the next day for 8 to 10 minutes, stirring occasionally.

Spread the desired amount of mayo on both sides of the toasted bread. Cover with the desired amount of shredded cabbage. Divide the jackfruit preparation among all the sandwiches. Top with cucumber slices, scallions and pickles to taste. Serve immediately. I like to drizzle a little lime juice on top. This is a slightly messy sandwich, so have napkins handy!

'FU-MAMI BROTH AND VEGGIES

In A Hurry

Umami and some heat? This one's got it all! Big flavors, fantastic textures and a fancy-looking outcome to boot. I'm hard-pressed to pick a favorite recipe, but this one is a strong contender.

YIELD: 4 servings

FOR THE TOFU

1 tbsp (15 ml) melted coconut oil or peanut oil

1 pound (454 g) super firm tofu, broken into 1-inch (2.5-cm) pieces

2 tbsp (40 g) Gochujang Paste (page 180) or store-bought

2 tbsp (30 ml) kimchi brine

1 tbsp (15 ml) reduced-sodium tamari

FOR THE BROTH

1 cup (235 ml) vegan lager beer (such as Sapporo) or vegetable broth

1 cup (235 ml) water

³/₄ cup plus 1 tbsp (195 ml) brewed Lapsang Souchong (1 teabag in hot water for 10 minutes)

1-1¹/₂ tbsp (20–30 g) Gochujang Paste (page 180) or store-bought

2 tbsp (30 ml) kimchi brine

2 tbsp (30 ml) reduced-sodium tamari

1 tsp (2 g) Easy as 2, 2, 2 Broth Mix (page 156)

1 tsp (2 g) dried shiitake powder (or 2 rehydrated shiitake caps, minced)

1 tsp (5 ml) toasted sesame oil

¹/₂ tsp grated fresh ginger root

1 clove garlic, grated

¹/₂ cup (96 g) drained Homemade Kimchi (page 27) or store-bought, chopped

¹/₂ cup (75 g) Japanese Carrot Pickles (page 189), chopped

1¹/₂ cups (201 g) fresh or frozen green peas, placed in boiling water for 1 minute until bright green

2 cups (80 g) packed fresh baby spinach, chopped

¹/₂ cup (40 g) thinly sliced scallions

2 small avocados, pitted, peeled and sliced

(continued)

To make the tofu, heat the oil in a large skillet on medium-high heat. Add the tofu and cook until golden brown, stirring occasionally and adjusting the heat as needed. This will take 8 to 10 minutes. While the tofu cooks, in a small bowl, whisk to combine the gochujang paste, kimchi brine and tamari. Add this mixture to the skillet during the last 2 minutes of cooking to glaze the tofu. Be careful of the splatter. Stir to combine and cook until absorbed. This can be prepared the day prior to making the rest of the recipe and stored in an airtight container in the refrigerator. Reheat in a pan before use, then cut into thin slices. Set aside.

To make the broth, in a large pot, whisk to combine the beer, water, tea, gochujang paste to taste, kimchi brine, tamari, broth mix, shiitake powder, sesame oil, ginger and garlic. Then add the kimchi and carrot pickles. Bring to a low boil, lower the heat and simmer for 2 minutes.

Divide the tofu among 4 bowls, reserving a few slices for garnish. Divide the peas, spinach and broth among the bowls. The spinach will wilt as the warm broth is poured on top. Top with the reserved tofu, scallions and avocado. Serve immediately.

MATCHA TEMPEH AND PICKLED VEGGIES SANDWICHES

If you're looking for the recipe that received the most praise during testing, you've found it. Described as "heavenly" and "the perfect definition of what umami is all about"—there's really nothing left to say!

YIELD: 4 sandwiches

FOR THE TEMPEH

3 tbsp (45 ml) lemon juice

1 tbsp (15 ml) brown rice vinegar or seasoned rice vinegar

1 tbsp (15 ml) grapeseed oil

1 tbsp (20 g) agave nectar

2 cloves garlic, grated

2½ tsp (5 g) matcha powder

½ tsp smoked sea salt

8 oz (227 g) tempeh, cut into 4 rectangles, then each rectangle cut into 2 thin rectangles

FOR THE QUICK PICKLES

3 tbsp (45 ml) brown rice vinegar

3 tbsp (45 ml) seasoned rice vinegar

3 tbsp (45 ml) water

1 tsp (3 g) coarse kosher salt

1 tsp (4 g) coconut sugar or other sugar

1 baby bok choy, trimmed and chopped

1 large carrot, thickly shredded

5 red radishes, thinly sliced

2 scallions, sliced

1 clove garlic, thinly sliced

FOR THE MAYO AND SANDWICHES

½ cup (114 g) regular flavor Faba-lous Mayo (page 167) or store-bought

½ tsp wasabi powder, or to taste

1½ tsp (8 ml) reduced-sodium tamari

1 clove garlic, grated

8 slices sourdough or whole grain vegan bread, lightly toasted

Fresh cilantro leaves (optional)

(continued)

MATCHA TEMPEH AND PICKLED VEGGIES SANDWICHES (CONT.)

To make the tempeh, in a shallow dish, whisk to combine the lemon juice, vinegar, oil, agave, garlic, matcha and salt. Coat each tempeh rectangle with the marinade, and marinate for at least 1 hour in the refrigerator. Preheat the oven to 375°F (190°C, or gas mark 5). Place the tempeh on a baking sheet lined with parchment paper. Bake for 8 minutes on each side. Set aside to cool slightly or completely.

To make the quick pickles, in a medium bowl, whisk to combine the vinegars, water, salt and sugar. Stir the bok choy, carrot, radishes, scallions and garlic into the mixture. Cover and let stand for 30 minutes in the refrigerator before use.

To make the mayo, whisk the mayo, wasabi, tamari and garlic in a small bowl until well combined. Adjust the quantity of wasabi to taste, as its strength varies with each brand.

To assemble the sandwiches, spread 1 tablespoon (14 g) of mayo on each slice of bread. Top 1 slice with 2 tempeh rectangles, the desired amount of drained pickled veggies and the cilantro (if using). Top with the second slice. Repeat with the remaining 3 sandwiches. Serve immediately.

ASIAN-INSPIRED FONDUE

Oil-Free

Here's a typical Swiss meal—with an Asian twist! If you don't want to dip bread cubes, simply toast slices of bread and spread the fondue on there. No one's judging your way of eating this fondue as long as you enjoy it.

Japanese Aomori black garlic is a delicacy that is fermented in pure sea water, making it sweet and mild. If you cannot find it locally, use roasted regular garlic instead to get the inimitable garlic flavor without the sharpness.

YIELD: 4 to 6 servings

---

1 cup (120 g) raw cashew pieces, soaked in 2 cups (470 ml) of filtered water for 6 hours, drained and rinsed

1 cup (235 ml) no- or low-sodium vegetable broth

1/4 cup (60 ml) vegan Japanese lager beer (such as Sapporo or Asahi)

1/4 cup (60 ml) unsweetened canned coconut cream

1/4 cup (48 g) drained Homemade Kimchi (page 27) or store-bought

3 tbsp (15 g) nutritional yeast

1 tsp (2 g) dried shiitake powder (or 1 rehydrated shiitake mushroom cap, minced)

1 1/2-2 tbsp (27-36 g) white miso, to taste

1/2 tsp Japanese Aomori black garlic (see headnote) or 2 cloves roasted garlic

1 tbsp (8 g) organic cornstarch

1 loaf crusty bread, cut into 1-inch (2.5-cm) cubes

Japanese Carrot Pickles (page 189) and Shichimi Togarashi (page 161), for serving (optional)

Place the cashews, broth, beer, coconut cream, kimchi, nutritional yeast, shiitake powder, miso, garlic and cornstarch in a blender. Blend until completely smooth and combined.

Transfer to a medium saucepan. Start on medium heat, then lower the heat to low and cook, whisking constantly, until thickened. This will take about 6 minutes. You want to be able to dip bread in the fondue without it being too thin or too thick. Turn off the heat and leave the fondue on the stove for another 6 minutes, whisking occasionally. If you have a fondue pot, you can skip that last step and just leave the pot over the candle while you're eating.

Spear a bread cube onto your fondue fork or regular fork, and swirl it in the mixture. Don't lose your bread or the drinks are on you! (Them's the rules.) Serve with carrot pickles and sprinkle with shichimi togarashi, if desired.

CARAMELIZED JACKFRUIT TACOS

Gluten-Free

Cooking your jackfruit in the oven, coated with a sweet and savory sauce, allows it to caramelize beautifully, boosts the flavors and causes a slight crispness at the edges. I highly recommend using the Peppers in a Pickle (page 176) as a topping here. They really do make these tacos even better!

YIELD: 8 tacos

2 (20-oz [567-g]) cans young green jackfruit in brine, drained, rinsed and shredded

1 tbsp (15 ml) grapeseed or olive oil

Scant 1 tbsp (8 g) minced fresh lemongrass

4 cloves garlic, peeled and minced

½ medium red onion, peeled and minced

2 tsp (13 g) agave nectar

2 tsp (10 ml) reduced-sodium tamari

3 tbsp (45 ml) Fish-Free Sauce (page 172)

Cracked rainbow peppercorn

1 cup (273 g) Savory Sweet Finishing Sauce (page 190)

1 recipe Lime-y Broccoli (page 98, broccoli part only)

8 (6-inch [15-cm]) corn tortillas

Garnishes: Fresh cilantro leaves, sliced scallions, Peppers in a Pickle (page 176)

Preheat the oven to 400°F (200°C, or gas mark 6). Line a large rimmed baking sheet with parchment paper or a silicone baking mat. In a large bowl, fold to combine the jackfruit with the oil, lemongrass, garlic, onion, agave, tamari, Fish-Free Sauce and peppercorn to taste. Place the jackfruit evenly on the prepared sheet.

Bake for 15 minutes. Use two rubber spatulas to stir and spread evenly. Bake another 15 minutes, then stir. Add the finishing sauce on top and stir to combine. Spread evenly and bake for another 15 minutes. Stir and bake for another 10 minutes, until caramelized but not overly dry. Be careful not to burn. Turn off the oven and leave the pan in the oven until ready to serve. While the jackfruit is baking, prepare the broccoli recipe.

Heat the corn tortillas so that they are pliable, then add a few florets of broccoli on top, along with about ⅓ cup (50 g) of jackfruit or whatever fits without falling out too easily. Top with cilantro, scallions and peppers to taste. Drizzle a little pickled pepper brine on top. Serve immediately.

There might be leftovers of jackfruit and broccoli. They can be stored in airtight containers in the refrigerator for up to 3 days, then gently reheated and served in the form of bowls with your grain of choice.

TERIYAKI TEMPEH TACOS

Gluten-Free • In A Hurry

Layered with Asian flavors and some mighty textural power, these will be perfect to help ring in the next Taco Tuesday! Frozen baby corn is so much tastier than canned, but it can be hard to find. If you cannot locate any, replace the baby corn with the same quantity of frozen corn kernels.

YIELD: 8 tacos

FOR THE RICE

1 cup (188 g) dry brown jasmine rice or other rice, cooked per package instructions with 1 tsp (5 ml) toasted sesame oil

1 tbsp (15 ml) brown rice vinegar

1 tsp (5 ml) ume plum vinegar

FOR THE TEMPEH

1½ tsp (8 ml) toasted sesame oil

1½ tsp (8 ml) reduced-sodium tamari

8 oz (227 g) tempeh, cut into bite-sized pieces

½ cup (120 ml) Teriyaki Sauce (page 175), divided

FOR THE VEGETABLES

1½ tsp (8 ml) toasted sesame oil

4 cloves garlic, peeled and minced

8 oz (227 g) fresh snow peas, trimmed and cut in two

1 red bell pepper, trimmed and chopped

⅔ cup (147 g) sliced frozen baby corn (see headnote)

¼ cup (65 g) sliced water chestnuts, chopped

FOR THE TACOS

8 (6-inch [15-cm]) corn tacos, heated to soften

½ cup (96 g) drained Homemade Kimchi (page 27) or store-bought, chopped (optional)

2 tbsp (14 g) roasted sesame seeds

Vegan Sriracha sauce

½ cup (40 g) sliced scallions

Toasted sesame oil

To make the rice, fluff the cooked rice and place in a bowl, gently folding with the vinegars. Set aside.

To make the tempeh, place the sesame oil, tamari and tempeh in a nonstick skillet. Sauté on medium-high heat for 2 minutes, stirring occasionally, and add ¼ cup (60 ml) of teriyaki sauce. Sauté on medium heat until glazed and golden, stirring occasionally, about 8 minutes. Set aside.

To make the vegetables, place the oil, garlic, snow peas, bell pepper and baby corn in a nonstick skillet. Sauté for 2 minutes. Add 3 tablespoons (45 ml) of teriyaki sauce and the water chestnuts, stir well and cook until tender but still crisp, about 4 minutes. Set aside.

To assemble the tacos, in the center of each tortilla, add 1 tablespoon (12 g) of rice, 2 tablespoons (20 g) of veggies, 1 tablespoon (12 g) of kimchi (if using) and 6 cubes of tempeh. Drizzle 1 tablespoon (15 ml) of teriyaki sauce over the filling. Top with sesame seeds, Sriracha to taste and scallions. Drizzle with sesame oil, fold and serve immediately. There will be leftover tempeh, rice and vegetables.

SMOKY KALE AND CHICKPEAS WITH MISO PEANUT DRIZZLE

Gluten-Free • In A Hurry

So quick and easy, this flavor-packed, smoky stir-fry is great served alone. It's also a perfect match with roasted sweet potatoes to make for a colorful complete meal. Or try it with the potatoes from Harissa Citrus Veggies (page 115). While definitely good for you, this dish is quite a treat too.

YIELD: 3 to 4 servings, 1 cup (235 ml) drizzle

FOR THE DRIZZLE

¹/₃ cup (85 g) natural peanut butter

1 tbsp (18 g) red miso, more if needed

Juice from 1 lemon (2 tbsp [30 ml])

2 tsp (10 ml) toasted sesame oil

2 tsp (13 g) agave nectar or brown rice syrup

2¹/₂ tbsp (15 g) chopped scallions

1 clove garlic, minced

1 tbsp (15 ml) brown rice vinegar or seasoned rice vinegar

¹/₃ cup (80 ml) water, more if needed

FOR THE KALE AND 'PEAS

2 tsp (10 ml) sesame oil

1 small red onion, chopped

1¹/₂ cups (256 g) cooked chickpeas

2 large cloves garlic, minced (to taste)

¹/₂ tsp smoked sea salt

¹/₂ tsp smoked paprika

¹/₄ tsp chipotle powder

1 large bunch kale (about 14 oz [397 g]), ribs removed, washed and chopped

(continued)

SMOKY KALE AND CHICKPEAS WITH MISO PEANUT DRIZZLE (CONT.)

To make the drizzle, place the peanut butter, miso, lemon juice, sesame oil, agave, scallions, garlic, vinegar and water in a blender. Blend until perfectly smooth. Adjust the miso to taste, and add more water if needed to get a thick yet pourable dressing. Set aside while preparing the rest of the dish. I like to use a squeeze bottle to serve the drizzle; it makes for a prettier presentation.

To make the kale and 'peas, place the sesame oil, onion, chickpeas, garlic, salt, paprika and chipotle powder in a large skillet. Heat on medium-high and stir-fry until the onion is golden brown and fragrant, about 4 minutes. Be sure to stir frequently to prevent scorching. Add the kale and cook until wilted, about 2 minutes. Serve with potatoes on the side, and drizzle peanut sauce on top. If there are sauce leftovers, store them in an airtight container in the refrigerator. It tastes great on tofu bowls, baked potatoes and roasted vegetables.

HOMEMADE KIMCHI

Gluten-Free • Oil-Free

Sure, you can buy vegan kimchi at most stores these days, but where's the fun in that?

I rarely leave anything to ferment longer than 24 hours due to the warm weather we almost always have in this corner of California, but timing will vary depending on location. Remember your kimchi will continue to ferment in the refrigerator, only at a far slower pace.

Now for a few safety notes: Make sure the utensils and equipment are sparkling clean to prevent the introduction of bad bacteria to your batch of kimchi. Wash your hands thoroughly and repeatedly during the process, wearing food-safe gloves to keep things clean and keep your hands from being exposed to ingredients that might irritate your skin. If your kimchi smells off at the end of fermentation, cry a little if you must and then toss it. Sadly, it can happen with fermented foods. Just pick yourself up and try again.

YIELD: Approximately 32 ounces (908 g)

---

1 head Napa cabbage (about 2 pounds [908 g]), outer leaves removed and cored

¼ cup (56 g) coarse kosher salt or (73 g) fine non-iodized sea salt

Filtered water, to cover

1 small (100 g) Asian pear (aka nashi fruit), peeled if not organic, cored and sliced

3 tbsp (45 ml) Fish-Free Sauce (page 172)

2-inch (5-cm) chunk daikon radish, peeled and thinly sliced

1 large carrot, trimmed, peeled and thickly shredded

5 scallions, trimmed and sliced

1 tbsp (9 g) minced garlic

1 tbsp (12 g) drained Pickled Ginger (page 175), minced

1 tbsp (18 g) white miso

1-4 tbsp (8-32 g) gochugaru (Korean red chile powder), to taste

Equipment: Sterilized 64-oz (1.9-L) food mason jar with airtight lid, 2 large bowls, large colander, wooden spoon

(continued)

HOMEMADE KIMCHI (CONT.)

Cut the cabbage in half and then into 2-inch (5-cm) chunks. Wash thoroughly, place in a very large bowl and cover with salt. Put food-safe gloves on and massage the salt into the cabbage. Add enough water to generously cover the cabbage, weighing it down with a plate if needed to submerge all leaves. Cover with a lid or plastic wrap, and let stand at room temperature for at least 4 hours or overnight. This will soften the cabbage and start the fermentation process.

Drain the cabbage and rinse it in several runs of water, making sure to rinse between the leaves as well. I like to place the cabbage in a large colander placed inside the rinsed bowl it was soaked in, and do 3 thorough rinses in a row to prevent the kimchi from being overly salty. Let drain for 30 minutes.

In the meantime, place the Asian pear, fish-free sauce, radish, carrot, scallions, garlic, ginger, miso and gochugaru in a large bowl. Wearing food-safe gloves, massage to thoroughly combine. Squeeze the cabbage slightly before adding to the bowl, and massage to coat well.

Transfer the cabbage to the mason jar, pressing down to pack with a clean spoon to make sure no air pockets remain. Leave at least 1 inch (2.5 cm) of space at the top of the jar. Seal with the lid, and let stand at room temperature for 24 to 36 hours. Be sure to place the jar in a bowl or on a plate as some of the brine might seep through the lid as the mixture ferments and bubbles.

Open the jar after 24 hours to check for doneness: it should smell pungent and taste sour. Use a clean spoon to press down and release air bubbles, and place the lid back on. Refrigerate now if it's ready. If not, leave it at room temperature for another 12 to 24 hours. Check and press down with a clean spoon again. Your batch of kimchi can be enjoyed now, but will benefit tremendously from spending at least another 4 days in the refrigerator. The longer it sits, the more its flavor will develop. Use within 1 month.

KINOKO GOHAN

In A Hurry

In Japanese, *kinoko* means mushroom and *gohan* means cooked rice. This dish is umami magic in its purest form. Traditionally, the mushrooms and other ingredients are all cooked together in a saucepan or rice cooker. My rice always seems to remain crunchy if I combine too much stuff with it as I cook it, and that's why I do things separately here. While not entirely authentic, this dish is fast, easy and a surefire umami win.

YIELD: 3 to 4 servings

---

1 recipe Mushroom Dashi (page 181, slow method, rehydrated mushrooms included)

1 cup (180 g) dry white jasmine rice, thoroughly rinsed and drained

2 tsp (10 ml) toasted sesame oil, divided

1 tbsp (15 ml) sake or brown rice vinegar

1 tbsp (15 ml) reduced-sodium tamari, or to taste

1 tbsp (18 g) white or red miso

2 cloves garlic, peeled and minced

4 small scallions, trimmed and sliced

$\frac{1}{3}$ cup (64 g) drained Homemade Kimchi (page 27) or store-bought, chopped

Garnishes: Shichimi Togarashi (page 161), roasted sesame seeds, crumbled nori sheet, lightly sautéed enoki mushrooms, shredded carrot

Combine the dashi (without the mushrooms), rice and 1 teaspoon (5 ml) of sesame oil in a rice cooker. Make sure you have enough liquid to cook the rice according to the brand you use. Usually, white jasmine rice calls for $1\frac{1}{2}$ cups (355 ml) liquid for every cup (160 g) of rice, which should be what the mushroom dashi recipe yields. If necessary, add extra water until you reach the required amount. Cook according to manufacturer's instructions. Alternatively, combine in a saucepot, cover with a lid, bring to a boil, lower the heat and simmer until the water is absorbed. Let stand covered for 10 minutes.

While the rice cooks, whisk to combine the vinegar, tamari and miso in a large bowl.

Slice the rehydrated shiitake mushrooms into thin strips, discarding stems if they are tough. Heat the remaining 1 teaspoon (5 ml) of oil in a medium skillet and sauté the mushrooms with the garlic, scallions and kimchi on medium heat to brown slightly, about 4 minutes. Stir occasionally while cooking. Transfer to the bowl, and gently fold to combine.

Transfer the cooked rice into the same bowl, and gently fold to combine. Serve immediately with garnishes of choice.

CHAZUKE (MATCHA-SOAKED RICE)

Gluten-Free • In A Hurry

What a great way to use leftover cooked rice! Chazuke is a Japanese dish made by pouring prepared matcha tea or, alternatively, dashi (page 181) over cooked rice.

YIELD: 3 servings

3 cups (about 585 g) cooked rice of choice

1½ cups (355 ml) Mushroom Dashi (page 181)

1 large clove garlic, grated

1 tbsp (12 g) drained Pickled Ginger (page 175), minced

½ tsp ume plum vinegar

½ cup (120 ml) hot but not boiling filtered water

1 tsp (2 g) matcha powder

1 tbsp (18 g) white miso

1 recipe Matcha Tempeh (page 15), prepared and baked

1½ cups (201 g) frozen green peas, thawed

Garnishes: Sliced scallions, Shichimi Togarashi (page 161) or Gomashio (page 109), Japanese Carrot Pickles (page 189)

Gently reheat the rice. Prepare the broth by whisking the dashi with the garlic, ginger and vinegar in a small saucepan. Bring to a low boil on medium-high heat, then remove from the heat.

In a small bowl, whisk the hot water with the matcha and miso. Whisk the miso preparation into the dashi.

Divide the rice and the peas among 3 bowls. Divide the broth among the bowls, using the amount you prefer. Usually you're aiming for about the same amount as the plant-based milk you'd add to your cold cereal. Top with crumbled slices of tempeh, scallions, shichimi togarashi or gomashio and carrot pickles. Serve immediately.

TAMARIND MISO SOUP

Gluten-Free • In A Hurry

The addition of sour tamarind paste here creates a sassy, slightly tangy, miso soup that can become the perfect lunch with baked tofu cubes and crispy baguette slices on the side. Alternatively, you can gently clean and reconstitute 2 dried shiitake mushrooms in ⅓ cup (80 ml) water, mince them and add them while sautéing the vegetables in this dish. This'll do the trick just fine. Be sure to keep the soaking water and replace the same quantity of water needed in this recipe with it. Don't you just love it when there is no waste?

YIELD: 2 to 3 small servings

---

1 tsp (5 ml) melted coconut oil or peanut oil

9 oz (255 g) baby bok choy, thinly chopped whites and roughly chopped greens (kept separate)

3 oz (85 g) trimmed and peeled young carrots, cut into matchsticks

3 cloves garlic, thinly sliced

3 cups (705 ml) water

3 tbsp (54 g) white miso

2 tsp (11 g) tamarind paste

2 tsp (3 g) dried shiitake powder (see headnote)

2 tsp (8 g) coconut sugar

1½ tsp (8 ml) reduced-sodium tamari

1 tsp (5 ml) toasted sesame oil

Generous ½ tsp ground ginger or 2 tsp (4 g) grated fresh ginger root

Garnishes: Sliced scallions, sliced daikon radish, roasted sesame seeds, chopped dry roasted unsalted peanuts, crumbled roasted nori sheet, pan-fried or roasted cubes of tofu

Place the oil, white parts of bok choy, carrots and garlic in a large pot. Sauté on high heat until tender-crisp, stirring frequently, about 6 minutes. Set aside.

In a medium saucepan, bring the water to a boil. Once boiling, turn off the heat. Place the miso, tamarind, shiitake powder, sugar, tamari, sesame oil and ginger in a small bowl. Carefully remove ¼ cup (60 ml) of boiling water. Whisk into the miso bowl, until thoroughly combined. Transfer this preparation into the hot water, then stir into the vegetable pot. Add the green parts of the bok choy and simmer just until wilted, about 2 minutes. Serve immediately with garnishes of choice.

QUICK AND EASY PAD THAI

Gluten-Free • In A Hurry

Granted, a few staples are needed here to make this outstanding dish quick and easy. But I'm ready to bet you'll have a constant stash of said staples in the refrigerator once you discover how they add such tremendous depth of flavor and make your meals a thousand times more awesome.

YIELD: 3 to 4 servings

¼ cup (60 ml) Mushroom Dashi (page 181)

1½ tbsp (18 g) coconut sugar

¼ cup (60 ml) Fish-Free Sauce (page 172)

2 tbsp (30 ml) fresh lime juice

2 tbsp (30 ml) rice wine vinegar

1 tbsp (15 g) tamarind paste

1 clove garlic, grated

½ tsp grated ginger root

1 bird's eye chile, seeded and minced

1 tbsp (15 ml) melted coconut oil or peanut oil

8 oz (227 g) tempeh, cut into bite-sized cubes

12 oz (340 g) chopped green cabbage

4 oz (113 g) brown rice stir-fry noodles, cooked according to package directions

Garnishes: Serundeng (page 171), lime wedges, fresh cilantro leaves, sliced scallions, reduced-sodium tamari

In a medium bowl, whisk the dashi with the sugar to dissolve the crystals. Add the Fish-Free Sauce, lime juice, vinegar, tamarind, garlic, ginger and chile. Whisk to combine and set aside.

In a large pot, heat the oil on medium-high heat. Add the tempeh and cook until golden brown, about 8 minutes. Adjust the heat as needed and stir frequently. Add the cabbage and cook until lightly browned, about 4 minutes. Add the sauce and simmer for a few minutes, until the sauce starts to thicken slightly and the cabbage is just tender, about 4 minutes. Add the cooked noodles and stir to coat the noodles well.

Serve with garnishes. Leftovers are even better, so the dish can be made ahead of time and reheated gently on the stove.

GOCHUJANG KIMCHI SAUSAGES

Somebody call the police because these vegan sausages stole all the umami amazingness in the world. They come in handy in the Gochujang Kimchi Bowls (page 41), Korean-Style Soft Tacos (page 42) and Kimchi Fried Rice (page 45). Consider making a double batch because they freeze really well, too!

YIELD: 6 sausages

2 tbsp (30 ml) reduced-sodium tamari

2 tbsp (30 ml) brown rice vinegar

2 tbsp (40 g) Gochujang Paste (page 180) or store-bought

4 rehydrated shiitake mushrooms (Reserve the soaking water)

⅓ cup (64 g) Homemade Kimchi (page 27) or store-bought

4 cloves garlic, grated

¼ cup (20 g) minced scallions (green and light green parts)

1 tbsp (18 g) red miso

2 tsp (10 ml) toasted sesame oil

½ cup (120 ml) Mushroom Dashi (page 181) with 1 tsp (2 g) Easy as 2, 2, 2 Broth Mix (page 156)

1 cup (144 g) vital wheat gluten

¼ cup (30 g) garbanzo flour

¼ cup (20 g) nutritional yeast

Prepare 6 (12-inch [30-cm]) pieces of foil, and get your steamer ready. Place the tamari, vinegar, gochujang paste, shiitake mushrooms, kimchi, garlic, scallions, miso, sesame oil and dashi in a food processor. Blend until smooth. Transfer to a large bowl. Add the gluten, flour and nutritional yeast on top. Stir with a rubber spatula and then switch to using one hand, kneading to thoroughly combine.

Divide the mixture into 6 equal portions of about 3 ounces (87 g) on the prepared foil. Shape into 6-inch (15-cm) sausages. Roll and wrap the foil tightly around each sausage, twisting the ends to enclose the mixture.

Steam the wrapped sausages for 75 minutes. Remove the foil carefully, and let the sausages cool to room temperature before storing in an airtight container in the refrigerator overnight. Brown in a bit of oil with extra gojuchang paste before use. See browning instructions on page 41.

GOCHUJANG KIMCHI BOWL

In A Hurry

I make this into a healthy, complete meal by serving it on top of cooked brown rice. It's also quite lovely with a generous squirt of Miso Peanut Drizzle (page 24) on top. If you find the gochujang paste a little too thick to glaze the sausages, you can dilute it in about 1 tablespoon (15 ml) of Mushroom Dashi (page 181) or low-sodium vegetable broth.

YIELD: 3 to 4 servings

2 tsp (10 ml) sesame or peanut oil

3 Gochujang Kimchi Sausages (page 38), sliced on the bias into 1/2-inch (1.3-cm) slices

2 1/2 tbsp (50 g) Gochujang Paste (page 180) or store-bought, divided, plus extra for serving

2 tsp (10 ml) melted coconut oil

2 heaping cups (270 g) julienned baby carrots

2 tsp (10 ml) reduced-sodium tamari

2 tsp (10 ml) brown rice vinegar

2 small heads fresh broccoli, trimmed and chopped

1/3 cup (64 g) Homemade Kimchi (page 27) or store-bought (brine included)

3 cloves garlic, peeled and minced

Mushroom Dashi (page 181) or low-sodium vegetable broth

Cooked brown rice, to serve

2 scallions, thinly sliced

Roasted sesame seeds (any color), for garnish

Heat the sesame oil on medium-high heat in a large skillet. Add the sausages and cook until browned, flipping occasionally to brown both sides. Adjust the heat as needed so that the sausages don't become dry. This will take approximately 4 minutes per side. Add 1 1/2 tablespoons (30 g) of gochujang paste (see headnote) and flip to coat the sausages, glazing for 1 to 2 minutes. Transfer to a plate and set aside.

In the same skillet, heat the coconut oil on medium-high. Add the carrots and cook until they just become tender, about 5 minutes. Deglaze with the tamari and vinegar, and add the remaining tablespoon (20 g) of gochujang paste, stirring to combine. Add the broccoli, kimchi and garlic. Cook until the broccoli is tender to taste, yet still bright green. Be sure to stir occasionally. Deglaze with the dashi as needed during cooking to keep the vegetables moist. Stir the sausages into the vegetables, and cook for another minute.

Serve on top of cooked rice to taste, and top with scallions and seeds. If you're daring, add extra gochujang paste to your portion.

KOREAN-STYLE SOFT TACOS

In A Hurry

I can't get enough of that spicy gochujang paste! If you're not a fan of peanut butter or can't eat it due to allergies, feel free to replace the peanut butter spread with mayo (page 167, or store-bought) to taste. If you use the mayo, you won't need the extra 2 teaspoons (10 ml) of lime juice.

YIELD: 8 tacos

---

1 tbsp (15 ml) sesame oil

2 Gochujang Kimchi Sausages (page 38), cut into ½-inch (1.3-cm) pieces on the bias, then halved

1 shallot (about 2 oz [56 g]), peeled, trimmed and minced

4 small cloves garlic, minced

2 small green bell peppers, cored and diced

2 tbsp (40 g) Gochujang Paste (page 180) or store-bought, plus extra for serving

1 tbsp plus 2 tsp (25 ml) lime juice, divided

⅓ cup (85 g) natural peanut butter, crunchy or creamy

½ English cucumber, cut into 2½-inch (6.5-cm) pieces, thinly sliced lengthwise with a mandoline slicer

2 sliced scallions

2 tbsp (30 ml) seasoned rice vinegar

1 tsp (5 ml) reduced-sodium tamari

8-inch (20-cm) vegan flour tortillas, heated to soften

Roasted sesame seeds and fresh cilantro leaves, for serving

Heat the sesame oil in a large skillet on medium-high. Add the sausages and shallot. Sauté to brown, stirring occasionally, about 4 minutes. Add the garlic and bell peppers. Sauté until the peppers are tender yet still crisp, about 3 minutes.

While the sausages and veggies are cooking, stir to combine the gochujang paste with 1 tablespoon (15 ml) of lime juice. Set aside.

Get your peanut butter to a stirrable consistency by heating it slightly if super thick or diluting it with a little bit of vegetable broth if needed. Stir to combine the peanut butter with the remaining 2 teaspoons (10 ml) of lime juice. Set aside.

Pour the gochujang mixture into the skillet, and stir to coat. Cook another minute and set aside.

In a medium bowl, stir to combine the cucumber slices, scallions, vinegar and tamari.

In the center of each warm tortilla, spread 2 teaspoons (10 g) of the peanut butter mixture. (For the extra daring among us, spread 1 to 2 teaspoons of extra gochujang paste along with the nut butter.) Top with ¼ cup (50 g) of the sausage-and-veggie filling. Top with a generous amount of cucumber and scallions. Top with sesame seeds and cilantro to taste, fold and eat.

KIMCHI FRIED RICE

In A Hurry

This one's a highly adaptable recipe and will mainly depend on the ripeness and spiciness of your kimchi. I recommend using a young, as in not super ripe, kimchi if you're going to use the full amount noted here. I used Homemade Kimchi (page 27) after about a week of preparation. If using super ripe kimchi, halve the amount and add tofu or extra veggies. You can also elect to add chopped and pan-fried Gochujang Kimchi Sausages (page 38) and extra tamari or gochujang if your kimchi really is on the weak side.

YIELD: 3 to 4 portions

2 tbsp (30 ml) melted coconut oil or peanut oil, divided

1 medium white onion, peeled, trimmed and chopped

1 pound (454 g) Homemade Kimchi (page 27) or store-bought, roughly chopped

1½ cups (201 g) frozen green peas

3 cups (will vary, 585 g) cooked and chilled rice of choice

1 tbsp (15 ml) reduced-sodium tamari

1 tbsp (15 ml) kimchi brine

Garnishes: Chopped dry roasted peanuts and sesame seeds, thinly sliced scallions, crumbled roasted nori sheet, mild-flavored fried or baked tofu of choice, Gochujang Kimchi Sausages (page 38)

Heat 1 tablespoon (15 ml) of oil on medium-high heat in a large skillet or wok. Add the onion and cook until it starts to brown, about 5 minutes. Stir occasionally. Add the kimchi and cook until it isn't too juicy anymore and is heated through, about 5 minutes. Add the green peas and cook until bright green and heated through, about 3 minutes. Set aside.

Break the rice apart with a spoon to remove clumps. In another skillet, heat the remaining 1 tablespoon (15 ml) of oil on medium-high heat. Add the rice to the oil and cook until heated through and crisp, about 3 minutes. Add the tamari and kimchi brine, and cook until absorbed and fragrant, about 2 minutes. Be sure to stir occasionally. Stir the rice into the vegetables to combine. Cook for another 2 minutes to let the flavors meld. Serve with your garnishes of choice.

FIVE-SPICE TERIYAKI BOWL

If you already know you are a fan of the warm, yet pungent, licorice-like flavor of five-spice powder, use the full 2 teaspoons (6 g) in this comforting bowl coated in umami-rich teriyaki sauce. I happen to live with a star anise and fennel hater, which are two of the components of the mix along with cardamom, cloves and Szechuan pepper. Good news: The hater in question really enjoys this dish.

YIELD: 4 servings

1½ tbsp (12 g) organic cornstarch

1¼ cups (295 ml) Mushroom Dashi (page 181), divided

1 tbsp (6 g) Easy as 2, 2, 2 Broth Mix (page 156)

½ cup (120 ml) Teriyaki Sauce (page 175)

4 tsp (20 ml) melted coconut or peanut oil, divided

1 pound (454 g) super firm tofu, cut into bite-sized cubes

Coarse kosher salt

1 heaping cup (120 g) thin carrot matchsticks

¼ cup (40 g) chopped white or yellow onion

1 heaping cup (110 g) chopped fresh broccoli

1 heaping cup (130 g) chopped fresh bell pepper (any color)

4 cloves garlic, peeled and minced

1½-2 tsp (4-6 g) Chinese Five-Spice Powder (page 162) or store-bought, to taste

9 oz (255 g) dry somen noodles or other noodles, cooked according to package directions

Garnishes: Thinly sliced scallions, red pepper flakes or vegan sriracha sauce, sesame seeds, fresh cilantro

Place the cornstarch at the bottom of a medium saucepan. Add 2 tablespoons (30 ml) of Mushroom Dashi on top, and whisk to dissolve. Add the remaining dashi, broth mix and teriyaki sauce. Whisk to thoroughly combine. Bring to a boil. Lower the heat, and simmer on medium heat until thickened to a molasses-like consistency, about 8 to 10 minutes. Stir occasionally and adjust the heat as needed.

Heat 2 teaspoons (10 ml) of oil in a large, deep skillet on medium-high heat. Add the tofu and a pinch of salt. Cook until golden brown on all sides, about 10 minutes, stirring occasionally and adjusting the heat as needed. After 6 minutes of cooking, add 3 tablespoons (45 ml) of the teriyaki mixture to the tofu, 1 tablespoon (15 ml) at a time, stirring to combine after each addition. It will moisten and flavor the tofu. Once the sauce is absorbed, transfer the tofu to a plate.

In the same skillet, heat the remaining 2 teaspoons (10 ml) of oil on medium-high heat. Add the carrots and onion, and cook until the carrots just start to become tender, about 4 minutes. Stir frequently. Add the broccoli and cook for 2 minutes, stirring frequently. Add the bell pepper, garlic and five-spice powder. Cook for 2 minutes or until all the veggies are tender to taste. Add the tofu back to the skillet.

Add the sauce on top of the veggies and tofu, and simmer to heat through, about 2 minutes. Divide the cooked noodles among 4 bowls, top with veggies and tofu and serve immediately with garnishes of choice.

ORANGE MARMITE NOODLE BOWL

In A Hurry

What is it about food in bowls? Maybe it's the fact you can hold your whole meal in the palm of your hand? Who knows, as long as it's as gobble-worthy as this one is. As a side note, use the amount of yeast extract you're most comfortable with: If you're new to it, go slow and add more as you make this dish again. If you already know your love for it is limitless, go for the full amount. Keep in mind that some yeast extracts are more intense than others. We're looking at you, Vegemite.

YIELD: 3 servings

---

2 tsp (5 g) organic cornstarch

¼ cup (60 ml) fresh orange juice (about 1 orange, add zest of half the orange before juicing)

¼ cup (60 ml) Mushroom Dashi (page 181)

1½ tbsp (23 ml) reduced-sodium tamari

1 generous tbsp–2 tbsp (28–40 g) yeast extract (such as Marmite, Vegemite or Cenovis), to taste

2 tbsp (40 g) agave nectar

1 tbsp (15 ml) melted coconut oil or peanut oil

8 oz (227 g) tempeh or super firm tofu, cut into bite-sized cubes

9 oz (255 g) shredded cabbage (both colors) and carrot

2 large cloves garlic, minced

1 small mild or hot pepper, seeded, cored and minced

3 individual bundles instant ramen (about 5 oz [150 g] total), cooked according to package directions

Shichimi Togarashi (page 161), for serving

Thinly sliced scallions, for serving

Place the cornstarch in a small saucepan and whisk to combine with the orange juice. Add the dashi, tamari, yeast extract and agave nectar. Whisk to combine. Alternatively, combine these ingredients with a blender if the yeast extract is extremely thick, as is often the case for Vegemite. Heat on medium-high heat and cook until it starts to thicken, about 4 minutes, whisking frequently. Set aside.

Heat the oil in a large skillet on medium heat. Add the tempeh cubes, and sauté until golden brown, about 6 minutes, stirring frequently. Add the cabbage, garlic and pepper. Sauté until just softened, about 4 minutes, stirring frequently. Add the yeast extract sauce, stirring to combine, and cook another minute.

Divide the cooked noodles among 3 bowls. Top with the tempeh preparation, Shichimi Togarashi to taste and scallions.

CRISPY THIN SAVORY PANCAKES

Gluten-Free

The flavor of these crêpe-like, crispy, rice flour pancakes reminds me of the rice wrappers used in fried spring rolls. They are great with any savory filling you can think of, but you really should try them with a Vietnamese-inspired mushroom filling (page 53) or with an Indonesian-style twist (page 105). Note that for best results, it's important to use a nonstick pan that's in good shape. I find that using an oversized, angled spatula also helps lift the pancake out of the pan with no breakage.

YIELD: 6 pancakes

1¼ cups (295 ml) filtered water

¼ cup (60 ml) unsweetened canned coconut milk or coconut cream

¼ cup (60 ml) Fish-Free Sauce (page 172)

1 cup (160 g) white rice flour (not sweet rice flour)

¼ cup (32 g) organic cornstarch

½ tsp dried shiitake powder

⅛ tsp Maldon sea salt

2 tbsp (30 ml) melted coconut oil, as needed

In a medium bowl, whisk to combine the water, coconut milk, Fish-Free Sauce, rice flour, cornstarch, shiitake powder and salt. Cover and let stand for at least 1 hour or refrigerate overnight. Whisk again before use. Bring back to room temperature for 1 hour if chilled overnight.

To cook the pancakes, heat 1 teaspoon (5 ml) of oil in an 11-inch (28-cm) nonstick frying pan over medium heat. Add a scant ½ cup (110 ml) of pancake batter, quickly tilting the pan to cover most of the surface.

Cover with a lid to ensure even cooking and minimal cracking. Cook until the edges and bottom are golden brown, about 8 minutes. Adjust the heat as needed. Carefully flip the pancake to cook the other side for 2 minutes. Fill as desired. Repeat with a second pancake, heating 1 teaspoon (5 ml) of oil each time and making sure to stir the batter with each batch. You should get 6 pancakes in all, but this amount may vary slightly.

CRISPY THIN SAVORY PANCAKES WITH MUSHROOM FILLING

Gluten-Free

This smoky, spicy, mushroom-and-cabbage preparation is the perfect way to fill super thin and crispy rice flour pancakes. If you use Sriracha sauce like some people use ketchup, you're going to want to add a healthy drizzle of it on these.

YIELD: 6 pancakes

1 recipe batter Crispy Thin Savory Pancakes (page 50) (Add ¼ tsp ground turmeric to the batter, if desired.)

1 tsp (2 g) Lapsang Souchong tea leaves

½ tsp ground ginger

½ tsp coarse kosher salt

½ tsp coconut sugar or other brown sugar

¼ tsp green or red Szechuan peppercorn or white peppercorn

¼ tsp Chinese Five-Spice Powder (page 162) or store-bought

1 tsp (5 ml) toasted sesame oil

¾ cup (90 g) minced carrot

1 medium shallot, trimmed, peeled and chopped

2 large cloves garlic, peeled and minced

8 oz (227 g) sliced baby bella mushrooms

1⅔ cups (145 g) chopped green cabbage

6 oz (170 g) rehydrated shiitake mushrooms (page 181)

1 tbsp (15 ml) reduced-sodium tamari

Garnishes: Thinly sliced scallions, chopped unsalted dry roasted peanuts, vegan Sriracha sauce, fresh cilantro leaves

(continued)

CRISPY THIN SAVORY PANCAKES WITH MUSHROOM FILLING (CONT.)

Be sure to read the instructions to prepare the pancake batter ahead of time.

Place the tea, ginger, salt, sugar, peppercorn and five-spice in a spice grinder. Grind until very finely ground. Set aside.

Place the oil in a large skillet. Add the carrots, shallot and garlic. Cook on medium-high heat for 2 minutes. Stir frequently during the whole cooking process. Add the mushrooms and cook until they're browned and the water is rendered, about 4 minutes. Add the cabbage, shiitake mushrooms and ground spices. Stir to combine and cook until the cabbage is tender yet still crisp, about 3 minutes. Deglaze with the tamari, cook for 1 minute and set aside.

Start cooking a pancake according to instructions on page 50. When the pancake is cooked, add the filling on top of one half of the pancake, just enough to cover generously without overfilling. Fold the pancake over the filling and serve carefully. Repeat with the remaining pancakes and filling. Be sure to whisk the pancake batter between each batch. Serve immediately with garnishes of choice.

There will be leftovers of the filling, which should be stored in an airtight container in the refrigerator for up to 3 days. I love to eat the filling on top of cooked rice with the same garnishes listed in this recipe. If you don't love leftovers as much as I do, you can double the pancake recipe or halve the ingredients for the filling here.

SOY POMEGRANATE-GLAZED BABY EGGPLANTS WITH DUKKAH

Gluten-Free

This is a fancy and healthy appetizer-style dish that's proven itself to be kid-friendly as well! If baby eggplants are hard to find, use the same weight of regular eggplant, sliced into rounds of the same thickness.

YIELD: 3 to 4 servings, scant 1/4 cup (34 g) dukkah

FOR THE DUKKAH

1 tsp (2 g) ground sumac

1 tsp (2 g) Harissa Dry Mix (page 166) or store-bought dry harissa

1/4 tsp dried oregano leaves

1/4 tsp coarse kosher salt, or to taste

1/2 tsp ground coriander

1/4 tsp onion powder

4 tsp (10 g) roasted white sesame seeds

4 tsp (8 g) chopped pistachios or pine nuts

FOR THE EGGPLANTS

6 baby eggplants (420 g in all), cut into approximately 1/3-inch (8-mm) slices (stems can be left for visual appeal)

2 tbsp (30 ml) Pomegranate Molasses (page 186)

2 tsp (10 ml) roasted pistachio, hazelnut or sesame oil

2 tsp (10 ml) reduced-sodium tamari

Thinly sliced scallions, for serving

(continued)

SOY POMEGRANATE-GLAZED BABY EGGPLANTS WITH DUKKAH (CONT.)

To make the dukkah, combine the sumac, harissa, oregano, salt, coriander, onion powder, sesame seeds and pistachios in a mortar. Use a pestle to gently crush the spices and nuts to release the flavors. Crush rather finely. Alternatively, you can use a mini food processor or coffee grinder to do this, but be careful not to overprocess as this could turn the mixture into a paste. This can be made in advance and stored at room temperature or in the refrigerator for up to 2 weeks.

To make the eggplants, place the eggplant slices in a 9 x 13-inch (23 x 33-cm) baking pan. In a small bowl, whisk to combine the molasses, oil and tamari. Lightly brush the marinade on all sides of each eggplant slice. Cover, and marinate for 1 hour in the refrigerator.

Heat a regular or electric grill to medium-high. Lightly brush the eggplant slices again with the marinade before placing on the hot grill. Grill until marks appear and the eggplant is just starting to get tender while remaining firm, about 4 minutes. Baste with marinade as needed. Flip the slices and grill on the other side until marks appear, about 4 minutes, until the eggplant is fork-tender. Baste with marinade as needed.

Remove the eggplant from the grill and sprinkle with dukkah and scallions to taste. Serve as an appetizer or side to dishes such as Middle Eastern-flavored chickpeas and couscous.

ROASTED FINGERLING POTATOES WITH WHITE BARBECUE SAUCE

Gluten-Free

Here, flavor-jammed roasted potatoes take a dive into a rich, brightly zippy sauce for the ultimate palate-pleasing dining experience.

YIELD: 2 to 3 servings, ½ cup (120 ml) sauce

FOR THE POTATOES

1 pound (454 g) small fingerling potatoes, scrubbed and halved

1 large bell pepper (any color), trimmed, cored and chopped

1 small serrano pepper, seeded if desired, minced (optional)

1 small red onion, peeled and chopped

4 cloves garlic, peeled and minced

2 tbsp (30 ml) vegan Worcestershire sauce

1 tbsp (15 ml) reduced-sodium tamari

1½ tsp (8 ml) toasted sesame oil

½–1 tsp (5 ml) liquid smoke, to taste

FOR THE SAUCE

½ cup (114 g) regular flavor Faba-lous Mayo (page 167) or store-bought

½ to 1 tbsp (8 to 15 ml) apple cider vinegar, to taste

½ tsp vegan Worcestershire sauce

¼ tsp smoked sea salt

1 small clove garlic, peeled and grated

Few pinches of cayenne pepper or drops of hot sauce

To make the potatoes, preheat the oven to 425°F (220°C, or gas mark 7). Line a 9 x 13-inch (23 x 33-cm) baking pan with parchment paper. Place the potatoes, bell pepper, serrano (if using), onion, garlic, Worcestershire sauce, tamari, sesame oil and liquid smoke in a large bowl. Stir to combine. Place the potatoes evenly on the baking sheet. Roast for 40 minutes or until the potatoes are fork-tender. If the potatoes brown too quickly before becoming tender, wear oven gloves and cover the pan with foil.

To make the sauce, whisk to combine the mayo, ½ tablespoon (8 ml) vinegar, Worcestershire sauce, salt, garlic and cayenne. Have a taste. Add more vinegar if you feel your taste buds can handle it. Cover, and refrigerate until ready to use. Serve, dipping the potatoes in the sauce.

SWEET POTATO FRIES WITH SRIRACHA KETCHUP

Gluten-Free

It's a little trickier to get sweet potatoes to yield a crispy outcome, but this recipe makes a good effort of it with oh-so-satisfying results. The dusting of mushroom-y salt is the perfect additional umami kick!

YIELD: 2 servings, scant ¾ cup (197 g) Sriracha ketchup

---

3 medium sweet potatoes (a little over 17½ oz [500 g]), peeled or unpeeled, cut into ¼-inch (6-mm) sticks

½ cup (136 g) organic ketchup

1-2 tbsp (15-30 g) vegan Sriracha sauce, to taste

2 tsp (12 g) white miso

Scant 1 tsp (4 ml) fresh lime juice

½ tsp toasted sesame oil

1 tsp-1 tbsp (7-20 g) agave nectar (optional)

1½ tbsp (18 g) potato starch or (12 g) organic cornstarch

2 tbsp (30 ml) grapeseed oil

2 tsp (3 g) dried porcini powder

½ tsp Maldon sea salt

Soak the potato sticks in water for 1 hour. This will help remove the extra starch and make for crisper potatoes.

While the potatoes soak, prepare the ketchup in a medium bowl by whisking the ketchup, Sriracha to taste, miso, lime juice and sesame oil. Have a taste and see if you want to add agave, up to 1 tablespoon (20 g) added 1 teaspoon (7 g) at a time. Cover and store in the refrigerator until ready to use. This will keep for 1 week.

Rinse the potatoes and drain them well for 30 minutes. Place them on paper towels. While the potatoes dry, preheat the oven to 400°F (200°C, or gas mark 6). Line two large rimmed baking sheets with parchment paper.

Place the potatoes in a large bowl. Sprinkle the potato starch on top. Cover with a plate and shake to coat all the potatoes thoroughly. Remove any excess starch (it shouldn't be visible). Wipe the bowl clean, and transfer the potatoes back to it. Drizzle grapeseed oil on top, cover with a plate and shake to coat. Place evenly on the prepared baking sheets. Do not overcrowd otherwise the potatoes will steam, not crisp up.

Bake for 15 minutes. Flip, making sure to place them back evenly. Exchange baking levels in the oven for even baking. Bake for another 15 minutes, or until the potatoes are browned and crisp. Don't hesitate to extend the cooking time for ultimate crispness, but don't let the fries burn. Turn off the oven, leave the door ajar and let cool for 15 minutes to further crisp up.

While the potatoes are finishing, prepare the porcini dusting by placing the powder and salt in a mortar and crushing the salt with a pestle. Place the fries in a large bowl. Sprinkle with mushroom salt to taste, and shake to coat. Serve immediately with ketchup for dipping.

SQUASH BLOSSOM PIZZA

This is a deliciously savory pizza made gorgeous with the use of squash blossoms. If you cannot find any at the market, replace them with any zucchini or summer squash of choice, thinly sliced into rounds. You will need approximately 1 large squash or 2 smaller to cover the surface; have extra handy just in case. I could see adding minced fresh rosemary, thyme, oregano or parsley on top of this. The sturdier herbs can be baked, while parsley would be best added only upon serving.

YIELD: 4 servings

$\frac{1}{4}$ cup (60 ml) grapeseed oil or olive oil

1 small white onion, trimmed and peeled, sliced to about $\frac{1}{4}$-inch (6-mm) thick

4 cloves garlic, peeled and smashed

1 tsp (2 g) Aleppo pepper flakes or $\frac{1}{2}$ tsp red pepper flakes (to taste), plus extra for serving

Pinch saffron threads (optional)

1 cup (120 g) raw cashew pieces, soaked in filtered water at room temperature for 4-6 hours

$\frac{1}{3}$ cup (80 ml) unsweetened canned coconut milk or coconut cream

4 oz (113 g) extra-firm silken tofu or unsweetened plain vegan yogurt

Juice from $\frac{1}{2}$ lemon (1 tbsp [15 ml])

$\frac{3}{4}$ tsp coarse kosher salt (if using regular salt, use half the amount)

1 tbsp (5 g) nutritional yeast

1 tbsp (12 g) white chia seeds

Cornmeal, for crust

1 pound (454 g) vegan pizza dough of choice

10 squash blossoms, washed and drained, stamen removed, halved lengthwise

Freshly ground peppercorn

Maldon sea salt

Place the oil, onion, garlic and pepper flakes in a small saucepan. Heat on medium-low heat, then lower the heat once the bulky ingredients start to sizzle slightly. Cook on low heat for 5 minutes until fragrant and the onion becomes translucent. Remove from the heat, add the saffron threads (if using) and infuse for 1 hour. Mince the garlic and set aside.

Drain and rinse the cashews. Place the coconut milk, tofu, cashews, lemon juice, salt and nutritional yeast in a food processor or high-speed blender. Process until smooth. Add the chia seeds and process a few times until slightly thicker. Set aside.

Preheat the oven to 450°F (232°C, or gas mark 8). Place a thin layer of cornmeal on a large baking sheet. Roll out the pizza dough as thin as you can into a rectangle, approximately 11 x 14 inches (28 x 36 cm). Lightly brush the whole surface with infused oil, including the edges. There will be leftovers of the oil, which can be used to stir-fry veggies or to flavor pasta or other grains. Store covered in the refrigerator for up to 1 week.

Top with a layer (not too thick) of cashew preparation. There will be leftovers, which can be used on a future pizza within a week. Store in an airtight container in the refrigerator.

Evenly place the halved squash blossoms on the surface. Top with the minced garlic and with onion slices scooped out from the infused oil with a fork. Bake until golden brown, about 16 minutes. Top with ground pepper, salt and extra Aleppo pepper flakes to taste. Serve immediately.

SAVORY ASIAN-FLAVORED GRANOLA

Sick of sweet stuff for breakfast? It happens to the best of us. Breakfast never sounded so good with this savory, Asian-flavored granola to be served on top of unsweetened plain vegan yogurt. Jazz it up even more with thin slices of Persian cucumber, baby tomatoes, thinly sliced scallions and any other garnishes you fancy.

YIELD: 3³/₄ cups (510 g)

---

¹/₄ cup (64 g) crunchy natural peanut, cashew or almond butter

2 tbsp (30 ml) melted coconut oil

2 tbsp (40 g) brown rice syrup

1¹/₂ tbsp (27 g) white miso

1 tbsp (12 g) coconut sugar

1 tbsp (15 ml) lemon juice

1 tbsp (15 ml) reduced-sodium tamari

2 tsp (3 g) nutritional yeast

1¹/₂ tsp (8 ml) toasted sesame oil

1¹/₂ tsp (8 g) vegan Sriracha sauce (to taste, optional)

2¹/₂ cups (240 g) rolled spelt flakes or (200 g) old-fashioned rolled oats

¹/₃ cup (40 g) raw cashew pieces

¹/₃ cup (37 g) unsalted dry roasted peanuts

Preheat the oven to 300°F (150°C, or gas mark 2). Line a large rimmed baking sheet with a silicone baking mat or parchment paper.

In a large bowl, whisk to combine the nut butter, oil, rice syrup, miso, sugar, lemon juice, tamari, nutritional yeast, sesame oil and Sriracha sauce (if using). Stir in the spelt flakes, cashews and peanuts to thoroughly coat.

Place the granola in an even layer on the prepared sheet. Bake until golden brown, about 30 minutes, carefully flipping with a large spatula approximately every 10 minutes. Take care not to break apart the clumps too much. Let it cool on the sheet; the granola will crisp up as it cools. Store in an airtight container in the refrigerator for up to 1 week.

LAPSANG SOUCHONG PINK PEPPERCORN SAVORY SHORTBREAD

Lapsang Souchong tea imparts a fantastic smokiness to everything it touches. I love it in this savory take on shortbread, matched with fruity, subtly spicy pink peppercorn. Note that each tea bag of the brand of Lapsang Souchong tea I use contains $1\frac{1}{2}$ teaspoons (3 g) of tea.

YIELD: 10 individual shortbreads

---

1 cup (120 g) whole-wheat pastry flour or all-purpose flour

$\frac{1}{4}$ cup (30 g) raw cashew pieces

1 tbsp (5 g) nutritional yeast

Slightly heaping $\frac{1}{2}$ tsp fine sea salt

2 tsp (10 ml) pure maple syrup

$3\frac{1}{2}$ tbsp (53 ml) melted coconut oil

3 tbsp (45 ml) water, divided, more if needed

1 tsp (2 g) coarsely ground pink peppercorn

1 tsp (2 g) Lapsang Souchong tea leaves

Preheat the oven to 350°F (180°C, or gas mark 4). Line a cookie sheet with parchment paper or a silicone baking mat.

Place the flour, cashews, nutritional yeast and salt in a food processor. Pulse until the cashews are finely ground. Add the maple syrup, oil and 2 tablespoons (30 ml) of water. Pulse to combine. The dough should be moist enough to hold together when pinched. If it isn't, add the remaining tablespoon (15 ml) of water and pulse until the dough reaches the proper moistness. Add extra water if needed, 1 teaspoon (5 ml) at a time after that.

Pulse the ground peppercorn and tea into the dough just twice to combine. Don't overdo it or the tea will turn the shortbreads a grayish hue.

Transfer the dough onto the parchment paper. Shape it into a log. Roll out the log into a $7\frac{1}{2}$ x 4-inch (19 x 10-cm) rectangle. Cut lengthwise into ten $\frac{3}{4}$-inch (2-cm) pieces. Use your hands to reshape each piece slightly. This will also help make for smoother edges once baked. Prick the top of each piece using the tines of a fork.

Arrange on the same parchment paper. Bake 18 to 20 minutes, until fragrant and light golden brown on the bottom and edges. Gently transfer to a cooling rack before having a taste. Store in an airtight container at room temperature for up to 3 days.

Chapter Two

SPICY

There's more than one way to go for spiciness! We're not only looking for piquant flavors here, but also for pungent, aromatic and zesty wonders.

You'll see all the spice mixes, sauces and pastes from the Staples chapter come to life in this chapter. Store-bought counterparts can be used if you are pressed for time or energy, and no one will blame you if you choose that option. This book is all about coaxing the very best flavors out of your food, of course, but convenience matters too.

If you're a little hesitant to work with fiery peppers, feel free to use less or even none at all. These recipes are entirely customizable to your own tastes and needs. Don't be afraid to get creative and make them your own. Go forth and be bold in the kitchen!

SUMMER PINTO BURRITOS

Whenever I write a cookbook, there's always a recipe that just wins above all others in my husband Chaz's view. You've guessed it: This one is it. Seeing his eyes light up—and the food devoured in no time at all—is possibly a bigger treat for me than actually eating the burritos myself! I hope your eyes light up when you try these, too.

YIELD: 6 burritos, ³⁄₄ cup (180 ml) dip

FOR THE DIP

¹⁄₂ cup (120 g) Simplest Nut-Free Cream (page 168)

¹⁄₄ cup plus 2 tbsp (90 ml) Spicy Citrus Sauce (page 179)

¹⁄₄ cup (20 g) minced scallions

Coarse kosher salt

FOR THE BURRITOS

³⁄₄ cup (180 ml) vegan lager beer

2 tsp (10 ml) olive oil or melted coconut oil

²⁄₃ cup (106 g) chopped red onion

¹⁄₂ bell pepper (any color), cored and chopped

2 tsp (11 g) double-concentrated tomato paste

1 tbsp (9 g) minced garlic

1 tsp (2 g) toasted cumin seeds, ground

¹⁄₂ tsp toasted coriander seeds, ground

1 tsp (5 g) maca powder or 2 tsp (3 g) nutritional yeast

¹⁄₂ tsp smoked sea salt

¹⁄₂ tsp chipotle powder

¹⁄₂ tsp ancho chile powder

2 tsp (10 ml) reduced-sodium tamari

1 roasted poblano pepper, cored, seeded and minced

1¹⁄₂ cups (256 g) cooked pinto beans

1 cup (160 g) cooked rice of choice

6 (10-inch [25-cm]) vegan flour tortillas, heated to soften

Garnishes: Sliced scallions, avocado slices, fresh cilantro leaves, and lime wedges

To make the dip, stir to combine the cream, citrus sauce, scallions and salt in a medium bowl. Cover and refrigerate until ready to use.

To make the burritos, place the beer in a small saucepan. Heat on medium-high to bring to a low boil, lower the heat and simmer until reduced to approximately half the original volume. You can eyeball this. It will take about 10 minutes. Set aside.

Heat the oil in a large skillet on medium-high heat. Add the onion, and sauté until lightly browned, about 4 minutes, stirring occasionally. Lower the heat to medium and add the bell pepper, tomato paste, garlic, cumin, coriander, maca, salt and chile powders. Cook for 2 minutes, stirring frequently. Add the reduced beer, tamari, poblano and beans. Simmer until the bell pepper is tender yet crisp, about 4 minutes.

Place 2 generous tablespoons (25 g) of cooked rice in the center of a tortilla. Add 6 tablespoons (75 g) of filling on top. Sprinkle with scallions to taste. Add avocado and cilantro, and fold burrito-style. I like to leave the top of mine open, as seen in the picture. Serve with lime wedges to drizzle.

PIRI PIRI PIT-ZA

This pizza is super simple, spicy and delicious. *Piri piri* means pepper pepper in Swahili, and this sauce is composed of hot peppers, citrus, lemon, onion, herbs and more. I use it as a kick-in-the-pants marinara on top of pita breads, with a little bit of cashew spread or vegan cream cheese to cool things down.

YIELD: 8 pit-zas, 1¼ cups (360 g) sauce

FOR THE SAUCE

1 large red bell pepper, cored and seeded

1 or 2 bird's eye chiles (to taste), cored and seeded

Generous handful sugar plum tomatoes (the equivalent of a medium regular tomato)

1 small red onion, trimmed, peeled and quartered

4 cloves garlic, peeled

½ tsp smoked sea salt

1 heaping tsp (3 g) smoked paprika

1 tsp (1 g) dried oregano leaves or 2 tsp (2 g) fresh oregano

2 tsp (11 g) double-concentrated tomato paste

1 tbsp (15 ml) olive oil or grapeseed oil

Juice from 1 lemon (2 tbsp [30 ml])

FOR THE PIT-ZAS

8 (8-inch [20-cm]) whole-wheat or regular vegan pita breads

½ cup (120 g) Cashew Spread (page 172) or store-bought vegan cream cheese

2 tsp (12 g) white miso

Toppings: Dried kalamata olives (pitted and chopped), soft sun-dried tomatoes (chopped), Peppers in a Pickle (page 176), thinly sliced mushrooms, fresh herbs

To make the sauce, place the bell pepper, chiles, tomatoes, onion, garlic, salt, paprika, oregano, tomato paste, olive oil and lemon juice in a food processor or blender. Process until combined and mostly smooth. Transfer to a large saucepan and heat on medium-high heat. Once the mixture starts to get bubbly, lower the heat and cook on medium-low for 30 to 35 minutes, stirring occasionally. Adjust the heat as needed. The mixture should lose most of its juices and be quite thick. Set aside.

To make the pit-zas, I like to use the broiler to do what follows, but you really must keep an eye on the pit-zas for it to work without scorching them. Alternatively, preheat the oven to 425°F (220°C, or gas mark 7). Place the pita breads on a baking sheet. Combine the spread with the miso, stirring well to thoroughly combine. Add 1 tablespoon (15 g) evenly on each pita bread. Top with 1½ tablespoons (27 g) of piri piri sauce. Apply the toppings that need to be cooked evenly on top of each pita bread.

If using the broiler, baking will take approximately 5 minutes. If using the regular oven, this will take approximately 10 minutes. Keep a close eye no matter which method you choose.

Serve immediately. There will be leftover piri piri sauce. Use it to make more pit-zas, or serve it with roasted potatoes, vegetables and more.

CRUNCHY CORN WAFFLES

These savory waffles are the perfect vehicle for Pineapple (or Mango!) Hot Pepper Jelly (page 194). They're also great with Citrusy Pepper Chili (page 116) or a big salad of mixed greens.

YIELD: 6 servings

1¼ cups (295 ml) unsweetened plain plant-based milk of choice

1 tbsp (15 ml) apple cider vinegar

1½ tsp (4 g) organic cornstarch

¼ cup (60 ml) water

1 generous tsp (8 g) smoked sea salt or fine sea salt

2 tbsp (24 g) Sucanat or organic light brown sugar

¼ cup (60 ml) grapeseed oil or olive oil

¼ cup (60 ml) fresh orange juice

1 cup (120 g) whole-wheat pastry flour or all-purpose flour

1 cup (160 g) organic medium-grind cornmeal

2 tbsp (10 g) nutritional yeast

2 tsp (9 g) baking powder

½ tsp baking soda

½ tsp chipotle powder

Nonstick cooking spray or oil spray

In a medium glass measuring cup, combine the milk with the vinegar and let stand 5 minutes to curdle.

In a small bowl, place the cornstarch and whisk with water to dissolve. Cook in the microwave for 30 seconds, or until cloudy and thickened to a jelly-like consistency. Don't overcook or the mixture will get clumpy. For guaranteed non-clumpy results, double the amount of cornstarch and water, cook 1 minute and use ¼ cup (50 g) of the mixture. Discard the rest. Alternatively, do this in a small saucepan over medium heat for about 2 minutes, stirring occasionally.

Whisk the cornstarch mixture, salt, Sucanat, oil and orange juice into the curdled milk. Sift the flour, cornmeal, nutritional yeast, baking powder, baking soda and chipotle powder on top of the wet ingredients, and briefly whisk to combine. Don't worry if a few lumps remain, just be sure not to overmix.

Let stand 15 minutes, and then preheat the waffle iron. The longer the batter sits, the better the outcome. Once the iron is hot, give a quick stir to the batter, generously coat the waffle iron with spray and cover the entire heating plate with batter, or follow the manufacturer's specific instructions. I get a total of 12 deep-pocketed, ¾-inch (2-cm) thick Belgian waffles on my iron, cooking 4 at a time. Cook until golden brown and crisp. It usually takes 8 full minutes on my waffle iron heated to 400°F (200°C).

Transfer to a cooling rack and repeat with the remaining batter. Reheat in a 325°F (170°C, or gas mark 3) oven until crisp again, about 10 minutes.

RED CHANA DAL MUJADDARA

Gluten-Free

Possibly the prettiest mujaddara you've ever made, this slightly sweet-and-sour twist on the Middle Eastern lentil, rice and fried onion dish boasts protein-rich chana dal (split baby chickpeas) and umami-filled sun-dried tomatoes. Note that the longer this dish marinates, the tastier it gets, which makes for great leftovers.

YIELD: 3 to 4 servings

---

1 tbsp (15 ml) melted coconut oil

1 medium red onion, diced

1 large red bell pepper, trimmed and diced

$^1/_4$ cup (28 g) minced soft sun-dried tomatoes (not in oil)

4 cloves garlic, minced

2 tsp (14 g) Harissa Paste (page 165) or store-bought, to taste

$^3/_4$ tsp smoked paprika

$^3/_4$ tsp ground coriander

2 tsp (3 g) nutritional yeast

2 tbsp (30 ml) reduced-sodium tamari, more to taste

$^3/_4$ cup (150 g) dry chana dal, rinsed and picked through, cooked

$^1/_2$ cup (90 g) dry jasmine or basmati brown rice, rinsed and picked through, cooked

$^1/_2$ cup (60 g) dry roasted almonds, coarsely chopped

2 tbsp (14 g) roasted sesame seeds (any color)

Pomegranate Molasses (page 186) or store-bought, for serving (optional)

Place the oil and onion in a large skillet. Cook on medium-high, stirring frequently, until the onion starts to caramelize, about 8 minutes. Lower the heat to medium and add the bell pepper. Sauté 2 minutes. Add the tomatoes, garlic, harissa, paprika, coriander and nutritional yeast. Sauté 1 minute to let the flavors develop. Add the tamari and the cooked chana dal and rice. Sauté 2 minutes or until the bell pepper is tender to taste, but still crisp. Remove from the heat, and leave at room temperature for at least 30 minutes to let the flavors develop. Serve with almonds, sesame seeds and a drizzle of pomegranate molasses (if using).

Serve immediately or store in an airtight container in the refrigerator. Gently simmer to reheat for about 8 minutes before serving.

RED CURRY VEGGIES

Gluten-Free • In A Hurry • Oil-Free

Have you noticed that different brands of red curry pastes vary wildly in heat and flavor? I bought one to make an earlier version of this curry and kept on having to add extra paste to get some semblance of flavor. It's like purchasing a small jar of nothingness! That's why I decided to make my own (page 185) for the most reliable results. Note that a few testers made this using the store-bought paste they're accustomed to. So fear not: It will work if you already have a favorite. You can always add more paste later, even after the coconut milk is added, so start with the lower amount of paste if you're not familiar with its intensity yet.

YIELD: 4 servings

2-3 tbsp (30-45 ml) reduced-sodium tamari, divided

9 oz (255 g) trimmed and cut green beans (1-inch [2.5-cm])

4 cloves garlic, thinly sliced

1 red onion, trimmed, peeled and diced

4 baby eggplants or 1 small eggplant (10 oz [283 g] total), trimmed and cut into thin half moons

1 bell pepper (any color), trimmed and chopped

1-3 tbsp (15-45 g) Red Curry Paste (page 185) or store-bought, to taste

2 tbsp (30 ml) lime juice

1 tbsp (5 g) dried shiitake powder

1/2 tsp ginger powder

1/2 tsp ground cumin

1/2 tsp ground coriander

1/2 tsp ground turmeric

1 (14-oz [414-ml]) can unsweetened coconut milk or coconut cream

1/2 tsp coarse kosher salt, or to taste

Cooked brown rice, legumes, potatoes, noodles or peas, for serving

Fresh basil or cilantro, for serving

Place 1 tablespoon (15 ml) of tamari, the green beans, garlic and onion in a large pot. Heat on medium-high and sauté for 2 minutes, stirring frequently. Add the eggplant and sauté until browned, approximately 4 minutes, stirring frequently.

Lower the heat to medium. Add the bell pepper, curry paste to taste, lime juice, shiitake powder, ginger, cumin, coriander and turmeric. Sauté 2 minutes to toast and release the flavors, stirring frequently. Add another 1 tablespoon (15 ml) of tamari and sauté for 1 minute.

Add the coconut milk, stir well and simmer until the veggies are tender to taste, about 8 minutes. Have a taste and add the salt if you feel it's needed.

Serve on top of rice or other choice of grain or potatoes. Add a chopped herb of choice, and adjust the amount of tamari to taste.

VERY TAHINI TEFFBALLS AND DRESSING

Gluten-Free

Here, a generous selection of warm spices mingles with gluten-free teff grain to create small, but mighty flavorful, nuggets. I love eating these finger food style-dipped in the dressing. They're also fantastic in pita bread with shredded lettuce, tomato, cucumber slices and a drizzle of the dressing on top.

YIELD: 30 teffballs, ³/₄ cup (180 ml) dressing

FOR THE TEFFBALLS

1 cup (200 g) dry teff grain

2¹/₄ cups (530 ml) water

1 jalapeño pepper, trimmed, cored and seeded if desired

1 cup (16 g) fresh cilantro leaves (not packed)

Scant ¹/₂ cup (45 g) chopped scallions

4 cloves garlic, minced

¹/₄ cup (64 g) roasted tahini paste

Juice from 1 large lemon (about 3 tbsp [45 ml])

2 tsp (10 ml) roasted pistachio, sesame or other oil

1 tsp (2 g) ground sumac

¹/₂ tsp fine sea salt

¹/₂ tsp ground turmeric

¹/₂ tsp ground coriander

¹/₂ tsp ground cumin

¹/₂ tsp Ras el Hanout (page 159) or store-bought

¹/₂ tsp smoked paprika

¹/₃ cup (50 g) minced bell pepper (optional)

¹/₄ cup (30 g) garbanzo bean flour

2 tbsp (30 ml) water

Nonstick cooking spray

FOR THE DRESSING

3 tbsp (48 g) tahini paste

¹/₃ cup (80 ml) water

2 tbsp (30 ml) lemon juice

4 tsp (20 ml) coconut cream

Pinch kosher salt

Pinch red pepper flakes

1 clove garlic, grated

(continued)

VERY TAHINI TEFFBALLS AND DRESSING (CONT.)

To make the teffballs, combine the teff and the water in a rice cooker. Cook covered until the water is absorbed. Let stand 10 minutes, then remove the lid and let cool slightly.

In a food processor, process the jalapeño, cilantro, scallions, garlic, tahini and lemon juice until finely chopped. Stop to scrape the sides with a rubber spatula once during the process. Transfer the mixture to a large bowl. Add the oil, sumac, salt, turmeric, coriander, cumin, ras el hanout and paprika. Stir to combine. Add the teff and stir to combine again. Cover and let cool to room temperature. Add the bell pepper (if using), flour and water, stirring to thoroughly combine, using one clean hand if needed. Cover and refrigerate for at least 2 hours or overnight.

In the meantime, make the dressing using a blender to thoroughly combine the tahini, water, lemon juice, coconut cream, salt, pepper flakes and garlic. Add extra water if needed, as the thickness of the tahini paste will vary. Cover and let stand at room temperature or in the refrigerator while baking the teffballs.

Preheat the oven to 375°F (190°C, or gas mark 5). You should get 30 teffballs in all, but the yield may vary. Lightly coat mini muffin tins accordingly with cooking spray. Grab 1 packed, heaping tablespoon (30 g) of mixture, roll it into a ball between the palms of your hands and place in the prepared tins.

Lightly coat the top of the bites with cooking spray before baking for 20 minutes. Remove from the oven and flip the teffballs. If you find they are a little fragile at this stage, let them stand 5 to 10 minutes before flipping the rest. Bake for another 10 to 15 minutes until firm. Let stand 10 minutes before serving with the dressing.

HASH AND SPICE

Gluten-Free

Here comes one of those dishes that tastes even better when reheated. So consider making it the day before for a great, filling, savory breakfast. Sacrilege alert: I roast the potatoes separately when making a hash to keep them cooked to perfection! If you are a purist, you can pan-fry the potatoes instead of roasting them. It'll take about the same amount of time, but you might have to add an extra tablespoon (15 ml) of oil if your skillet isn't well seasoned or nonstick.

You can double the potato recipe if you like a lot of potatoes in your hash. You can also replace the bell peppers with any vegetable you like; zucchini or carrots are great here. About 2 to 2½ cups (weight will vary) of chopped veggies will do the trick to replace the peppers.

YIELD: 4 servings

FOR THE POTATOES

1 tbsp (15 ml) grapeseed oil or other neutral-flavored oil

2 tbsp (30 ml) lime juice

½ tsp ground cumin

½ tsp smoked paprika

½ tsp onion powder

½ tsp smoked sea salt

1 pound (454 g) russet potatoes, cut into bite-sized cubes

FOR THE VEGGIES

2 tbsp (30 ml) lime juice

1 tbsp (15 ml) adobo sauce from a can of chipotle peppers

1 tbsp (17 g) double-concentrated tomato paste

½ tsp ground toasted cumin

½ tsp ancho chile powder

½ tsp smoked sea salt

1 tbsp (15 ml) grapeseed oil or other neutral-flavored oil

1 small red onion, peeled, trimmed and chopped

8 oz (227 g) sliced baby bella mushrooms

2 bell peppers (any color), cored and chopped

1 red Fresno pepper or other mild to hot pepper, cored and minced

2 large cloves garlic, peeled and minced

1½ cups (256 g) cooked pinto beans

Optional garnishes: Simplest Nut-Free Cream (page 168) or store-bought vegan sour cream, avocado or guacamole, Hash Spice (page 158), fresh parsley

(continued)

To make the potatoes, preheat the oven to 425°F (220°C, or gas mark 7). Line an 8-inch (20-cm) baking pan with a piece of foil. Place the oil, lime juice, cumin, paprika, onion powder and salt in the pan. Stir to combine, then add the potatoes and fold until well coated. Bake for 30 minutes or until fork-tender, stirring every 10 minutes. While the potatoes are baking, prepare the other veggies.

To make the veggies, in a small bowl, stir to combine the lime juice, adobo sauce, tomato paste, cumin, ancho powder and salt. Set aside.

Heat the oil on medium-high heat in a large skillet. Add the onion, and sauté until translucent, about 4 minutes. Be sure to stir occasionally throughout the cooking time and with each addition. Add the mushrooms and cook for 4 minutes, or until they're slightly browned and their moisture is released. Add all of the peppers and garlic. Cook until the peppers just start to soften, about 4 minutes. Add the beans and stir, cooking for another minute. Stir the sauce into the veggies, and cook another 4 minutes.

Divide the potatoes on plates. Serve topped with veggies, optional sour cream or avocado, and a liberal amount of hash spice and parsley.

HARISSA SPROUTS AND CHICKPEAS

Gluten-Free • In A Hurry

This sweet, savory and spicy concoction belongs served atop any cooked whole grain of choice to make it a fiber-rich, nourishing and absolutely delicious meal. It's also great with pita bread or chips and glazed nuts (page 137).

YIELD: 2 to 3 servings

---

2 tsp (10 ml) melted coconut or olive oil

1 pound (454 g) fresh Brussels sprouts, trimmed and quartered

1 large shallot, peeled and minced

1 large clove garlic, peeled and minced

Coarse kosher salt

1 tbsp (15 ml) Pomegranate Molasses (page 186), plus more for serving

1 tbsp (20 g) Harissa Paste (page 165) or store-bought, to taste

2 tbsp (32 g) tahini paste (use a pourable one)

1½ tsp (8 ml) reduced-sodium tamari

1½ tsp (8 ml) lemon juice

1½ tsp (10 g) agave nectar

½ tsp Harissa Dry Mix (page 166) or store-bought

1½ cups (256 g) cooked chickpeas

Roasted pistachio oil, for serving (optional)

Heat the oil on medium heat in a large skillet. Add the Brussels sprouts, shallot, garlic and a couple of pinches of salt. Sauté until golden brown and the sprouts are starting to become fork-tender, stirring frequently. This will take about 10 minutes, depending on the size and freshness of the sprouts.

While the sprouts are cooking, whisk to combine in a small bowl the pomegranate molasses, harissa paste, tahini, tamari, lemon juice, agave and harissa dry mix.

When the sprouts are just getting fork-tender, add the chickpeas and sauté another 2 minutes. Pour the harissa mixture on top and fold to combine. Cook for another 2 minutes. Serve with a tiny drizzle of pistachio oil (if using) and extra pomegranate molasses.

CHICKPEA-NUT CROQUETTES

These small croquettes are bursting with spicy personality. If you cannot find roasted peanut flour, lightly toast old-fashioned rolled oats in a pan and process in a grinder until finely ground. Use the same amount as roasted peanut flour.

YIELD: 24 croquettes

1½ cups (256 g) cooked chickpeas

4 cloves garlic, coarsely chopped

½ cup (50 g) coarsely chopped scallions

¼ cup (6 g) packed fresh cilantro leaves

¼ cup (64 g) natural crunchy peanut butter

1 tbsp (5 g) nutritional yeast

1 tbsp (15 ml) fresh lime juice

1 tbsp (15 ml) reduced-sodium tamari

2 tsp (10 g) sambal oelek

1½ tsp (8 ml) toasted sesame oil

½ tsp coarse kosher salt

½ tsp ground cumin

½ tsp ground coriander

1 medium carrot, trimmed, peeled and shredded

⅓ cup (25 g) panko bread crumbs, more if needed

⅓ cup (40 g) roasted peanut flour or toasted oat flour (see headnote)

Nonstick cooking spray or oil spray

Place the chickpeas, garlic, scallions, cilantro, peanut butter, nutritional yeast, lime juice, tamari, sambal oelek, sesame oil, salt, cumin and coriander in a food processor. Pulse until thoroughly combined, stopping twice to scrape the sides with a rubber spatula. The mixture should remain just slightly chunky.

Transfer this mixture to a large bowl. Add the carrots, bread crumbs and flour, using a rubber spatula to thoroughly combine. The mixture should hold together easily when pressed, without being too moist or too dry. If it is overly moist, add up to 3 tablespoons (15 g) of extra bread crumbs, 1 tablespoon (5 g) at a time.

Lightly coat two standard muffin tins with cooking spray. Alternatively, and for easier flipping, simply place the croquettes on a large baking sheet lined with parchment paper. Use 1 packed tablespoon (25 g) of mixture per croquette and shape into a slightly flattened ball. Place into the prepared muffin tins.

Repeat with the remaining mixture. You should get 24 croquettes in all. Lightly coat the croquettes with cooking spray. Cover with plastic wrap and store in the refrigerator for at least 1 hour, up to overnight.

Preheat the oven to 375°F (190°C, or gas mark 5). Remove the plastic wrap. Bake for 15 minutes and carefully flip. Lightly coat with cooking spray, and bake for another 10 to 15 minutes or until golden brown and firm. Let stand 10 minutes, then serve with Asian-Style Peanut Salad (page 91) or salad of choice.

ASIAN-STYLE PEANUT SALAD

Gluten-Free • In A Hurry

This crisp and refreshing salad is the ideal pairing to Chickpea-Nut Croquettes (page 88)! You might find yourself needing to double the yield the next time you plan on making it, it's that snackable.

YIELD: 2 servings

1 tbsp (15 ml) seasoned rice vinegar or brown rice vinegar

2 tsp (10 ml) toasted sesame oil

1 tsp (5 g) sambal oelek

1 tsp (5 ml) reduced-sodium tamari

1 tsp (5 ml) ume plum vinegar

$\frac{1}{2}$ tsp grated ginger root

1 to 2 scallions (to taste), trimmed and thinly sliced

1 clove garlic, grated

2 carrots (any color), trimmed and peeled

2 Persian cucumbers or summer squashes, trimmed

$\frac{1}{4}$ cup (37 g) dry roasted peanuts, coarsely chopped

2 tbsp (2 g) fresh cilantro leaves

In a medium bowl, whisk to combine the rice vinegar, sesame oil, sambal oelek, tamari, ume plum vinegar, ginger, scallions and garlic.

Shave the carrots and cucumbers lengthwise using a vegetable peeler or a mandoline slicer. Watch your fingers if using the latter! Add to the dressing, gently folding to combine. Alternatively, drizzle the dressing on top of the vegetables upon serving. Top with peanuts and cilantro.

ROASTED CABBAGE SLICES WITH CHERMOULA AND CHICKPEAS

Gluten-Free • Soy-Free

When you cut the head of cabbage, you should get 4 slices and leftovers from the sides of the cabbage. It might be wise to have a second head of cabbage handy in case your slices don't hold together well. Use caution when slicing. Reserve the leftover cabbage for other recipes, such as Quick and Easy Pad Thai (page 37). The freshness of the herbs combined with delicious garlic and zippy lemon make the chermoula the perfect accompaniment to virtually any dish.

YIELD: 4 servings, 1 scant cup (195 g) chermoula

FOR THE CHERMOULA

1 cup (70 g) lightly packed fresh parsley leaves and thin stems

1 cup (20 g) lightly packed fresh cilantro leaves and thin stems

1/3 cup (10 g) lightly packed fresh mint leaves

1 small jalapeño pepper, trimmed and seeded (optional)

2 cloves garlic, quartered

1 tsp (2 g) Aleppo pepper flakes

1/2 tsp sweet paprika

1 tsp (2 g) cumin seeds, lightly toasted and finely ground

1 tsp (2 g) coriander seeds, lightly toasted and finely ground

1/2 tsp coarse kosher salt, or to taste

1/4 cup (60 ml) lemon juice (about 2 medium lemons)

1/3 cup (80 ml) grapeseed oil or olive oil

FOR THE VEGETABLES

1 1/2 cups (256 g) cooked chickpeas, patted dry

1/2 tsp coarse kosher salt

1 tbsp (15 ml) melted coconut oil or other oil, plus extra to brush cabbage slices

1/2 tsp ground sumac

1/2 tsp Ras el Hanout (page 159) or store-bought

1 small green cabbage, cut into 1/2-inch (1.3-cm) slices

Maldon sea salt flakes or other salt

3/4 cup (128 g) dry quinoa, rinsed and cooked

1/4 cup (34 g) dry roasted pine nuts or pistachios

Garnishes: Fresh herbs, Aleppo pepper flakes, lemon wedges

(continued)

ROASTED CABBAGE SLICES WITH CHERMOULA AND CHICKPEAS (CONT.)

To make the chermoula, place the parsley, cilantro, mint, jalapeño (if using) and garlic in a blender or food processor. Process to chop. Add the pepper flakes, paprika, cumin, coriander and salt. Pulse a couple of times. Add the lemon juice and process again, drizzling the oil in as the machine works. Alternatively, this step can be done with a mortar and pestle in several batches. Transfer to an airtight container, cover and store in the refrigerator until ready to use. It's best to use the chermoula within a day. Stir before use.

To make the vegetables, preheat the oven to 375°F (190°C, or gas mark 5). Combine the chickpeas with the salt and oil. Place in an even layer in a 9-inch (23-cm) baking dish and bake for 30 minutes, stirring once halfway through. Toss the chickpeas with the sumac and ras el hanout. Set aside.

Raise the oven heat to 400°F (200°C, or gas mark 6). Line a baking sheet with parchment paper or a silicone baking mat. Place the cabbage slices onto the paper, lightly brushing each side with oil. Sprinkle a tiny pinch of salt on one side of each slice facing up. Bake until golden brown and the core is tender, about 25 minutes.

To assemble, place chermoula to taste at the bottom of a plate, brushing it to cover some of the plate surface. Top with a cabbage slice; be careful when transferring because these can be a bit fragile. Add the quinoa divided into 4 portions, chickpeas divided into 4 portions and 1 tablespoon (9 g) of pine nuts each. Top with garnishes of choice and serve with extra chermoula.

MOROCCAN-FLAVORED STUFFED SQUASH

Gluten-Free

There is so much flavor packed into something as small as a squash in this recipe! While the filling isn't overly spicy, it still has a bit of a kick. If you are sensitive, replace ¼ cup to ⅓ cup (60 to 80 g) of the Harissa Spread with the same quantity of fire-roasted crushed tomatoes. Also note that if you use store-bought ras el hanout, adjust the quantity to taste depending on the heat. If the mix contains salt, adjust the quantity of salt as well.

YIELD: 4 servings

---

2 tbsp (30 ml) Pomegranate Molasses (page 186)

2 tsp (10 ml) reduced-sodium tamari

4 tsp (20 ml) roasted pistachio oil, peanut oil or sesame oil, divided

1 tbsp (6 g) Ras el Hanout (page 159) or store-bought, divided

½ cup (60 g) walnut halves

4 summer squashes of choice (I used a little over 2 pounds [940 g] of Mexican squash)

2 large carrots, trimmed, peeled and minced

¼ cup (40 g) minced shallot

3 cloves garlic, minced

½ tsp smoked sea salt, or to taste

1½ cups (256 g) cooked chickpeas

1 cup (240 g) Harissa Paste (page 165)

Fresh mint leaves or parsley, for serving

Avocados, for serving (optional)

Preheat the oven to 300°F (150°C, or gas mark 2). In a small bowl, whisk to combine the molasses, tamari, 2 teaspoons (10 ml) of oil and 1 teaspoon (2 g) of ras el hanout. Add the walnuts to the bowl of molasses mixture and stir to combine. Remove the walnuts with a fork, letting the excess drip back into the bowl. Set the bowl aside for later use. Transfer the walnuts to a small baking pan lined with parchment paper, and bake until dry and toasted, about 10 minutes, flipping once halfway through. Set aside to cool.

(continued)

MOROCCAN-FLAVORED STUFFED SQUASH (CONT.)

Increase the oven heat to 425°F (220°C, or gas mark 7). Halve the squashes lengthwise, and hollow each half out but don't go too close to the skin so as not to break the shell. Chop the flesh you removed and set aside.

Lightly brush each shell inside and out with the molasses mixture. There might be leftovers of the mixture; set aside if that's the case. Place the squashes in a 9 x 13-inch (23 x 33-cm) baking pan, and bake until fork-tender, about 18 minutes. Set aside.

In a large skillet, heat the remaining 2 teaspoons (10 ml) of oil on medium heat. Add the carrots, reserved chopped squash flesh, shallot, garlic, salt and remaining 2 teaspoons (4 g) of ras el hanout. Cook until the carrots start to soften, about 6 minutes, stirring frequently. Add the chickpeas and cook for another minute. Add the harissa spread and stir to thoroughly combine. Cook for another 4 minutes.

Fill each squash shell with the chickpea preparation. If there is leftover molasses mixture, drizzle it on top. Top with chopped walnuts and chopped mint leaves. Serve with chopped or sliced avocado if desired.

RED CURRY SCRAMBLE WITH LIME-Y BROCCOLI

Gluten-Free • In A Hurry

Who says simplicity can't be outstanding? Here's edible proof that that couldn't be further from the truth. Virtually every vegan has one or two go-to tofu scramble recipes, and this spicy take on it, composed of everyday ingredients and paired with perfectly seasoned broccoli, is bound to become a new favorite.

Use the leftover canned coconut milk to make Miso Caramel (page 143), Marmite Peanut Halva (page 153), Asian-Inspired Fondue (page 19) or other recipes that use a partial can of coconut milk or coconut cream.

YIELD: 3 servings

FOR THE SCRAMBLE

1 tbsp (15 ml) grapeseed oil or other neutral-flavored oil

1 pound (454 g) super firm tofu, crumbled

1 generous tbsp (25 g) Red Curry Paste (page 185) or store-bought

2 tbsp (10 g) nutritional yeast

1 tbsp (15 ml) reduced-sodium tamari

1 tbsp (15 ml) unsweetened canned coconut milk or coconut cream

2 tbsp (30 ml) vegetable broth

FOR THE BROCCOLI

1 large head broccoli, trimmed and chopped (about 17 oz [482 g])

2 tbsp (30 ml) dried red chile-soaking water or vegetable broth

Zest and juice from 1 organic lime (2 tbsp [30 ml]) (Grate the zest prior to juicing!)

2 tbsp (30 ml) unsweetened canned coconut milk or coconut cream

Maldon sea salt or other flaky salt

Thinly sliced scallions

To make the scramble, heat the oil on medium-high heat in a large skillet. Add the tofu, and cook until browned all over, stirring occasionally. This will take up to 10 minutes depending on the tofu used. In a small bowl, combine the curry paste, nutritional yeast, tamari, coconut milk and broth. Pour the mixture onto the browned tofu, and cook down another 2 minutes.

To make the broccoli, cook on medium-high heat along with the chile water and lime juice until tender, stirring occasionally. This will take about 8 minutes, depending on the broccoli. Add the coconut milk and stir to combine, cooking another minute until the coconut milk is mostly absorbed.

Serve the scramble immediately, topped with the broccoli and lime zest, a pinch of Maldon salt, to taste, and scallions.

FRESH CORN TACOS WITH SALSITA VERDE

Gluten-Free • In A Hurry • Soy-Free

These tacos are filling, healthy, relatively quick to make and bursting with the kind of fresh flavors that make for the most unforgettable, vegetable-rich meals.

YIELD: 8 tacos, 1½ cups (350 g) salsa

FOR THE SALSA

5 tomatillos, husk removed, quartered

⅓ cup (6 g) packed fresh cilantro sprigs

1 large clove garlic, minced

½ tsp smoked sea salt

1 small jalapeño, cored and seeded, if desired, coarsely chopped

3 scallions, trimmed, chopped

FOR THE CORN

2 tsp (10 ml) olive oil

1 small red onion, chopped

3 cloves garlic, minced

2 ears corn, kernels scraped off

1 yellow or green bell pepper, trimmed and diced

½ tsp smoked sea salt

½ tsp ground cumin

½ tsp smoked paprika

½ tsp chipotle powder

FOR THE TACOS

8 (6-inch [15-cm]) fresh corn tortillas, heated to soften

2 large avocados, pitted, peeled and sliced

Garnishes: Cilantro leaves, toasted pepitas, Hash Spice (page 158), lime and lemon wedges

To make the salsa, combine the tomatillos, cilantro, garlic, salt, jalapeño and scallions in a food processor. Pulse until combined but still slightly chunky. Cover and refrigerate until ready to serve.

To make the corn, place the oil and onion in a skillet. Cook on medium-high until the onion browns slightly, about 4 minutes. Stir frequently. Add the garlic, corn, bell pepper, salt, cumin, paprika and chipotle powder. Stir-fry on medium-high heat until the pepper softens but remains crisp, about 4 minutes. Set aside.

To assemble the tacos, place about 3 tablespoons (36 g) of the corn preparation in the center of the tortilla. Top with salsa to taste. Top with avocado, cilantro leaves, toasted pepitas and sprinkle with hash spice to taste. Serve with citrus wedges alongside.

HARIRA (MOROCCAN SOUP)

Gluten-Free • Soy-Free

This soup is loaded with warm spices, healthy amounts of natural fiber and great flavors, of course. *Harira* is amazing served with pita bread and hummus. But then again, what isn't?

Start with the lower amount of harissa if you're not familiar with its heat level. You can always add a little extra upon serving if needed.

YIELD: 6 to 8 servings

1¹/₂ tbsp (23 ml) grapeseed oil or olive oil

2 medium carrots, trimmed, peeled and minced

1 medium red onion, trimmed, peeled and chopped

4 ribs celery heart, chopped

4 large cloves garlic, minced

1¹/₄ cups (111 g) chopped leek

1 small jalapeño pepper, trimmed, seeded and minced (optional)

8 oz (227 g) chopped baby bella mushrooms

1-2 tbsp (20-40 g) Harissa Paste (page 165) or store-bought, to taste

3 tbsp (49 g) double-concentrated tomato paste

2¹/₂ tsp (5 g) Ras el Hanout (page 159) or store-bought

¹/₂ tsp Tunisian Baharat (page 162)

¹/₂ tsp ground ginger

¹/₄ tsp ground turmeric

³/₄ tsp coarse kosher salt (adjust to taste, especially if store-bought ras el hanout contains salt)

1 tbsp (8 g) Easy as 2, 2, 2 Broth Mix (page 156)

¹/₂ cup (90 g) dry red lentils

28 oz (794 g) fire-roasted crushed tomatoes, with juice

28 oz (828 ml) water

1¹/₂ cups (256 g) cooked chickpeas

1-2 tbsp (15-30 ml) lemon juice, to taste

¹/₂ cup (8 g) fresh cilantro leaves, chopped

¹/₂ cup (8 g) fresh parsley leaves, chopped

Dry roasted pine nuts, for garnish

Place the oil, carrots, onion, celery, garlic, leek and jalapeño (if using) in a large pot. Heat on medium-high and cook for 4 minutes. Add the mushrooms, and cook until their moisture is released, about 4 minutes. Stir frequently during the cooking process.

Add the Harissa Paste, tomato paste, Ras el Hanout, baharat, ginger, turmeric, salt and broth powder. Stir to combine and cook for 1 minute. Add the lentils, tomatoes, water and chickpeas. Bring to a boil, reduce to a simmer and cook for 20 minutes or until the lentils are tender. Stir occasionally. Add the lemon juice and stir to combine.

Serve topped with fresh herbs and pine nuts. This stew tastes great served with pita and hummus, or try it with steamed potatoes. Store cooled leftovers in an airtight container in the refrigerator for up to 3 days.

INDONESIAN-INSPIRED RICE PANCAKES

Gluten-Free

Packed with many succulent flavors and textures, these pancakes are more reminiscent of French crêpes than American pancakes. This is definitely a fork-and-knife type of dish, so don't attempt to pick them up taco-style to eat!

YIELD: 6 pancakes

FOR THE INFUSED OIL

$^1/_4$ cup (60 ml) grapeseed oil or peanut oil

$^1/_2$-inch (1.3-cm) piece peeled fresh ginger root

1 clove garlic, left whole

2 tbsp (20 g) shallot, chopped large

1-inch (2.5-cm) stick pounded fresh lemongrass

2 bird's eye chiles, trimmed, halved and seeded

FOR THE PANCAKES

1 recipe batter Crispy Thin Savory Pancakes (page 50)

$1^1/_2$ tbsp (24 g) natural salted crunchy or creamy peanut butter

$1^1/_2$ tbsp (23 ml) rice wine vinegar

1 tbsp (15 ml) reduced-sodium tamari

2 tbsp (30 ml) infused oil

3 oz (85 g) rice noodles (mai fun), cooked according to package directions

$^1/_4$ cup (40 g) Japanese Carrot Pickles (page 189)

1 bell pepper (any color), cored, seeded and sliced

Sambal oelek

$1^1/_2$ cups (105 g) thinly shredded red cabbage

$^1/_4$ of an English cucumber, sliced

2 scallions, trimmed and sliced

Garnishes: Fresh cilantro leaves, Serundeng (page 171), lime wedges

To make the infused oil, place the oil, ginger, garlic, shallot, lemongrass and chiles in a small saucepan. Heat on medium-low, then lower the heat once the bulky ingredients start to sizzle slightly. Cook on low heat for 5 minutes. Remove from the heat and let cool before transferring to an airtight container to infuse overnight. Scoop out the bulky ingredients before using the oil; mince them for use in stir-fries or any other recipe.

To make the pancakes, be sure to read the instructions on page 50 to prepare the pancake batter ahead of time. Whisk the peanut butter, vinegar, tamari and infused oil in a medium bowl. Add the cooked noodles, carrot pickles and bell pepper to the infused oil dressing, tossing to combine. Set aside. Cook a pancake according to directions. Transfer to a plate, spread a small amount of sambal oelek on the whole surface if desired, top with $^1/_4$ cup (18 g) of the shredded cabbage, $^1/_6$ of the prepared noodles and veggies, a few slices of cucumber, scallions to taste and garnishes of choice. Fold the pancake and serve immediately. Repeat with the remaining pancakes.

SUMMER PLATE WITH PICKLED PEPPER CREAM

A tasty pairing of some of my favorite recipes from this book: a slight variation on these eggplants (page 55), walnuts (page 95) and gomashio (page 109). This stuff belongs in a soft flatbread, pita bread or simply served with crackers, but I just love to eat it as is on a pretty plate—kind of a fresh, spirited starter to whet the appetite.

YIELD: 2 to 3 servings

$^{1}/_{4}$ cup (60 ml) Pomegranate Molasses (page 186)

4 tsp (20 ml) roasted walnut oil or other oil

4 tsp (20 ml) reduced-sodium tamari

1 tsp (3 g) za'atar spice

$^{3}/_{4}$ cup (90 g) raw walnut halves

11 oz (311 g) trimmed baby eggplants cut into $^{1}/_{3}$-inch (6-mm) slices, or $^{1}/_{3}$-inch (6-mm) slices regular eggplant

1 small red onion, trimmed and peeled, halved and sliced thickly

$^{1}/_{2}$ cup (110 g) Simplest Nut-Free Cream (page 168) or store-bought

2 tsp–1$^{1}/_{2}$ tbsp (8–18 g) slightly drained Peppers in a Pickle (page 176), minced, to taste, plus extra for serving

Coarse kosher salt

20 grape tomatoes, halved

Gomashio (page 109) or store-bought

Fresh parsley leaves

Line a baking sheet with parchment paper or a silicone baking mat. Place the molasses, oil, tamari and za'atar in a 9 x 13-inch (23 x 33-cm) baking pan. Whisk to combine. Add the walnuts and stir to combine. Remove the walnuts from the marinade with a fork, letting the excess drip back into the pan. Transfer the walnuts to the prepared baking sheet.

Add the eggplant and onion to the molasses mixture and soak on both sides. Marinate for 1 hour in the refrigerator, flipping the slices once halfway through to make sure the slices all get bathed in the marinade.

While the eggplants marinate, preheat the oven to 300°F (150°C, or gas mark 2). Bake the walnuts until dry and toasted, about 10 minutes, flipping once halfway through. Set aside to cool. Chop once cooled, keeping the prepared baking sheet handy to bake the eggplant.

Increase the oven heat to 400°F (200°C, or gas mark 6). Remove the eggplant and onion from the marinade with a fork. Place the slices evenly on the prepared sheet. Bake until golden brown and tender but not mushy, about 10 minutes on each side. Baking time will vary depending on the freshness of the eggplant and size of the slices, so pay close attention. Remove from the oven. Chop the eggplant and onion into bite-sized pieces.

In a small bowl, whisk to combine the cream with the minced pickled veggies. Adjust the seasoning to taste. Decoratively spread the desired amount of cream on a plate. Top with the chopped eggplant and onion, tomatoes, walnuts, gomashio and parsley to taste. Add extra pickled veggies if you really like spice. Alternatively, serve in a soft flatbread, pita bread or with crackers.

TAHINI HARISSA TOAST WITH GOMASHIO

Soy-Free

This is like avocado toast made a thousand times better. I've kept things not too spicy, focusing on depth of flavor instead. Note that if you are using store-bought harissa, remember to adjust the quantity to taste as heat does vary with brand.

YIELD: 8 toasts, ¼ cup (28 g) gomashio, 1½ cups (350 g) spread

FOR THE GOMASHIO

¼ cup (28 g) raw sesame seeds (any color or a mix)

1 tsp (6 g) Maldon sea salt or other flaky salt (to taste)

FOR THE HARISSA SPREAD

1½ tsp (8 ml) roasted walnut oil or other oil

⅓ cup (50 g) minced shallot

1 large clove garlic, peeled and minced

1½ cups (360 g) fire-roasted crushed tomatoes

2 generous tbsp (50 g) Harissa Paste (page 165) or store-bought

1 tbsp (16 g) tahini paste

1 tbsp (15 ml) Pomegranate Molasses (page 186)

Coarse kosher salt

FOR THE TOAST

Tahini paste, as needed

8 small to medium slices of sourdough, lightly toasted

2 ripe but firm, small to medium avocados, halved, pitted, peeled and sliced

Pomegranate Molasses (page 186), for serving

Aleppo pepper flakes or Urfa pepper flakes (optional)

(continued)

TAHINI HARISSA TOAST WITH GOMASHIO (CONT.)

To make the gomashio, lightly toast the sesame seeds on low heat in a skillet, stirring to prevent burning. Once the seeds pop and are fragrant, let cool slightly, then transfer to a mortar and pestle with the salt. Coarsely grind to extract flavor, being careful not to turn it into a paste. Set aside.

To make the spread, heat the oil in a small saucepan on medium heat. Add the shallot and garlic and sauté until translucent, about 4 minutes. Be sure to stir frequently. Add the tomatoes, harissa, tahini and Pomegranate Molasses, stirring to combine, and lower the heat to a simmer. Simmer until thickened to a caramelized, paste-like consistency, about 45 minutes. As the spread cooks down, use a rubber spatula to stir almost constantly to prevent burning and spitting. Season to taste. Set aside to cool to room temperature before use, or refrigerate in an airtight container once cooled.

To assemble the toasts, spread a thin layer of tahini on still-warm toasts. Top with 1 tablespoon (15 g) of spread. Top with slices of the equivalent of a quarter avocado. Drizzle with a little molasses, and sprinkle gomashio and Aleppo pepper flakes (if using) on top. Serve immediately. Store leftovers in airtight containers in the refrigerator (spread) or at room temperature (gomashio) for up to 1 week. The remaining spread is used in Moroccan-Flavored Stuffed Squash (page 95).

SAVORY CURRY FARINA (UPMA)

In A Hurry

Quick to cook, healthy and so comforting, *upma* is the meal I turn to when I need something to eat now. It is a common breakfast dish in India, made from dry roasted semolina cooked into a porridge. I rarely serve savory food for breakfast, so I usually eat this farina-based version as a light evening meal instead. I like to eat a lot of kale with it, but you could definitely enjoy it with a different vegetable of choice and even add roasted chickpeas for a complete meal.

If you prefer a lower-fat option, feel free to replace the oil used to cook the kale with 1 tablespoon (15 ml) of vegetable broth instead. Simply add the kale and broth directly to the pot and start cooking.

YIELD: 3 to 4 servings

FOR THE KALE

1 tbsp (15 ml) melted coconut oil or other oil

1 pound (454 g) kale leaves, ribs removed

$1/2$ tsp ground turmeric

$1/2$ tsp smoked paprika

$1/2$ tsp smoked sea salt or other salt

FOR THE FARINA

1 cup (164 g) uncooked brown rice farina or whole-wheat farina

1 tbsp (15 ml) melted coconut oil or other oil

1 medium red onion or shallot, trimmed, peeled and chopped

2 cloves garlic, minced

1 tbsp (15 g) Red Curry Paste (page 185) or store-bought

2 tbsp (10 g) nutritional yeast

$1/2$ tsp ground cumin

$1/2$ tsp ground coriander

$1/2$ tsp ground turmeric

1 tbsp (15 ml) reduced-sodium tamari

$2^{1}/_{2}$ cups (590 ml) water or vegetable broth, more if needed

$1/2$ cup plus 2 tbsp (75 g) dry roasted cashew pieces

Thinly sliced heirloom tomatoes, fresh cilantro leaves, lemon slices, for serving

(continued)

SAVORY CURRY FARINA (UPMA) (CONT.)

To make the kale, heat the oil in a large pot on medium-high heat. That's a lot of kale before it cooks down, so be sure to use a really large pot. Add the kale and cook until it starts to wilt, about 2 minutes. Stir occasionally. Lower the heat to medium. Add the turmeric, paprika and salt, stirring to combine. Cook until the kale is completely wilted and tender, about 4 to 6 minutes; timing will depend on how sturdy the kale is.

To make the farina, in a dry medium pot, toast the farina on medium heat until fragrant and starting to turn a light golden brown, about 4 minutes. Adjust the heat as needed and be sure to stir frequently to prevent burning. Let it cool a couple of minutes, then transfer to a bowl.

Heat the oil in the same pot on medium-high heat. Add the onion and cook until browned, about 4 minutes. Stir occasionally. Lower the heat to medium. Add the garlic, curry paste, nutritional yeast, cumin, coriander and turmeric. Stir to combine. Add the toasted farina, and cook another minute. Add the tamari and water, and cook until the liquid is absorbed, about 6 minutes, stirring frequently. Adjust the heat as needed. Let stand for 5 minutes before serving.

Fluff the farina before serving with the kale. Top with cashews or stir some into the upma directly and add other garnishes to taste.

HARISSA CITRUS VEGGIES

Gluten-Free

I originally prepared this dish to part ways with vegetables languishing in the produce drawer of the refrigerator. But it turns out I was so pleased with the hearty results that I'm glad I took notes so that it could be shared. While I know not everyone is a huge fan of unrefined coconut oil, I urge you to use it with the potato part; working in combination with the other ingredients, it gives an almost cheesy flavor to the roasted tubers.

YIELD: 4 servings

FOR THE POTATOES

28 oz (794 g) cubed potatoes of choice (A combination of russet and sweet potatoes is great here)

2 tbsp (30 ml) melted coconut oil

2 tsp (4 g) Harissa Dry Mix (page 166) or store-bought

2 tbsp (30 ml) reduced-sodium tamari

FOR THE VEGETABLES

1 tbsp (15 ml) melted coconut oil or other oil

1 medium red onion, trimmed and chopped

2 large (13 oz [380 g] total) yellow squashes or zucchini, trimmed and chopped

3 cloves garlic, peeled and minced

2 small bell peppers (any color), cored and chopped

1 jalapeño pepper, seeded and trimmed

2 tsp (4 g) Harissa Dry Mix (page 166) or store-bought

1 tbsp (15 ml) reduced-sodium tamari

1²/₃ cups (434 g) fire-roasted crushed tomatoes

¼ cup (60 ml) Spicy Citrus Sauce (page 179)

1½ cups (256 g) cooked black-eyed peas

Sliced avocado and scallions, for serving (optional)

To make the potatoes, preheat the oven to 425°F (220°C, or gas mark 7). In a large bowl, stir to combine the potatoes, oil, harissa and tamari. Transfer to a baking sheet lined with parchment paper or a silicone baking mat. Bake until the potatoes are golden brown and tender, about 30 to 40 minutes depending on freshness and size. Flip the potatoes every 10 to 15 minutes for even browning.

While the potatoes bake, cook the vegetables. Heat the oil in a large pot on medium-high heat. Add the onion, squashes and garlic. Cook until lightly browned, about 4 minutes, stirring frequently. Add the peppers, and cook another 2 minutes. Add the harissa, and cook 1 minute while stirring. Add the tamari to deglaze, then add the tomatoes and citrus sauce. Stir to combine. Add the black-eyed peas and lower the heat to a simmer. Simmer for 10 minutes or until the vegetables are tender to taste. Adjust the seasoning to taste.

Serve the vegetables with the roasted potatoes. Top with sliced avocado and scallions, if desired.

CITRUSY PEPPER CHILI

Gluten-Free • In A Hurry

Rest assured that this chili is spicy in the sense that it's full of flavors and various spices, but it doesn't pack a punch in the way of heat. Unless you want it to, that is. Feel free to add extra heat sources, such as jalapeño pepper rings upon serving!

YIELD: 4 to 6 servings

1¹/₂ cups (355 ml) fresh tomato sauce

1¹/₄ cups (295 ml) vegetable broth

3 tbsp (45 ml) Spicy Citrus Sauce (page 179), plus more for serving

1 roasted red bell pepper, peeled, cored and seeded

2 tsp (10 ml) grapeseed oil

1 cup (160 g) diced white onion

1¹/₂ bell peppers (any color), cored and chopped

2 tsp (11 g) double-concentrated tomato paste

2 tsp (10 ml) reduced-sodium tamari

¹/₂ tsp ground cumin

¹/₂ tsp chipotle powder

¹/₂ tsp ancho chile powder

¹/₂ tsp ground cardamom

¹/₂ tsp smoked sea salt

¹/₂ tsp smoked paprika

2 tbsp (10 g) nutritional yeast

1¹/₂ tbsp (8 g) dried shiitake powder (or 4 rehydrated shiitake mushroom caps, minced)

4 cloves garlic, peeled and minced

1 packed tbsp (10 g) minced soft sun-dried tomatoes (not in oil)

1 roasted poblano pepper, peeled, cored and seeded

2 ears corn, cut from cob and roasted

1¹/₂ cups (256 g) cooked black beans

Place the tomato sauce, vegetable broth, citrus sauce and roasted bell pepper in a blender. Blend until smooth. Set aside.

Heat the oil in a large pot on medium-high heat. Add the onion and sauté until lightly browned, about 4 minutes, stirring occasionally. Add the peppers and sauté for 4 minutes. Add the tomato paste, tamari, cumin, chile powders, cardamom, salt, paprika, nutritional yeast, shiitake powder, garlic, sun-dried tomatoes and poblano pepper. Sauté for another 2 minutes, stirring frequently.

Add the corn and beans, as well as the tomato sauce mixture. Bring to a low boil. Lower the heat, and simmer uncovered for 10 minutes or until thickened to taste.

The chili tastes even better reheated the next day. Serve with extra citrus sauce if desired, along with your favorite garnishes, such as roasted pepitas, sliced scallions and avocado cubes. I like to enjoy mine on top of cooked quinoa; it makes for the perfect complete, filling-yet-light summer meal.

SUMMER SALAD BOWL WITH CITRUS DRESSING

Gluten-Free

This salad makes for an ideal light summer lunch or side dish, composed of crunchy and colorful fresh vegetables, paired with a zippy citrusy dressing. Please see the vegetable list used here as a guideline, and choose any combination of in-season vegetables that tempts you the most. Raw golden beets are far more tender than their red counterpart and add a nice, almost juicy, crunch here. Since beets are less earthy-tasting when used raw, they are also far better received by beet haters.

YIELD: 4 servings, scant ½ cup (100 ml) dressing

---

3 tbsp (45 ml) grapeseed oil

3 tbsp (45 ml) seasoned rice vinegar

3 tbsp (45 ml) Spicy Citrus Sauce (page 179)

2 tsp (13 g) agave nectar, or to taste

1 tbsp (10 g) minced shallot

Pinch coarse kosher salt, Aleppo pepper flakes and ground sumac

3 endives, trimmed, washed, gently spun dry and chopped

4 baby yellow beets, trimmed and peeled, cubed small

10 red radishes, trimmed and thinly sliced

9 oz (255 g) ready-to-eat fresh edamame, rinsed and drained

¾ cup (90 g) dry roasted walnut halves, coarsely chopped

Fresh flat-leaf parsley leaves, chopped

Whisk the oil, vinegar, citrus sauce, agave, shallot, salt, Aleppo pepper flakes and sumac in a small bowl to emulsify. Whisk again before serving if needed. Store leftovers in the refrigerator in an airtight container for up to 4 days, whisking before use again.

Divide the endive, beets, radishes and edamame among 4 bowls. Drizzle with dressing to taste, and top with walnuts and parsley. Serve immediately.

TIKKA MASALA POPCORN

Gluten-Free • In A Hurry • Soy-Free

Spicy, crunchy and deliciously tongue-tingling, this unusually flavored popcorn will be the perfect companion for catching up on your favorite TV shows. You can share it if you really must. If you want a lighter dusting of spice, feel free to double the recipe for the popcorn itself.

YIELD: 4 servings

FOR THE SPICE MIX

1$\frac{1}{2}$ tsp (3 g) nutritional yeast

1 tsp (5 g) dried tomato powder

1 tsp (3 g) garam masala

$\frac{1}{2}$–1 tsp (3 g) coarse kosher salt, to taste

$\frac{1}{2}$ tsp Sucanat or organic light brown sugar

$\frac{1}{4}$ tsp ground coriander

$\frac{1}{4}$ tsp regular or smoked paprika

$\frac{1}{8}$–$\frac{1}{4}$ tsp cayenne pepper, to taste

$\frac{1}{4}$ tsp dried onion powder

$\frac{1}{4}$ tsp dried garlic powder

$\frac{1}{8}$ tsp ground turmeric

FOR THE POPCORN

1 tbsp (15 ml) melted coconut oil or olive oil

$\frac{1}{4}$ cup (48 g) organic popping corn

Oil spray, as needed

To make the mix, place the nutritional yeast, tomato powder, garam masala, salt, Sucanat, coriander, paprika, cayenne pepper, onion powder, garlic powder and turmeric in a spice grinder. Grind finely to combine. Set aside.

To make the popcorn, place the oil in a large, heavy-bottomed pot fitted with a lid. Add 3 kernels of popping corn. Place the lid on the pot. Heat on medium heat, and wait until the kernels pop. Be sure to adjust the heat as needed so as not to burn the corn. Add the remaining kernels once the kernels pop, cover again and shake until the popping stops.

Transfer the popcorn to a large bowl. Remove any unpopped kernels. Spritz the popped corn with a little oil and slowly add the spice mix, shaking to make sure the popcorn is evenly coated. Serve immediately.

WELL-DRESSED CASHEW WHEELS

Gluten-Free

With a consistency similar to chèvre cheese and wrapped in a flavor-packed coating, even omnivorous guests can't resist diving cracker-first into these. It's important to allow time for the wheels to sit in the fridge so that the flavor can develop. Make these at least 5 days ahead of eating for the best results.

YIELD: 3 cashew wheels

Toasted nut oil of choice, for the ramekins

1 cup (120 g) raw cashews, soaked overnight, drained and rinsed

1¼ cups (295 ml) unsweetened plain cashew or other nut milk

¼ cup (60 g) unsweetened canned coconut cream (scooped from the top of an unshaken, chilled can of full-fat coconut milk stored in the refrigerator for 24 hours before use)

2 tbsp (30 ml) lemon juice

1 tbsp (18 g) white miso

1½ tsp (4 g) coarse kosher salt

1 tbsp (8 g) agar powder

¼ cup (32 g) Shichimi Togarashi (page 161) or (30 g) finely ground Dukkah (page 55)

Lightly brush 3 ramekins (4 inches [10 cm] in diameter) with oil. Set aside.

Place the cashews, milk, cream, lemon juice, miso and salt in a blender (or use an immersion blender), and blend until completely smooth. If you'd like, you can also let this mixture sit covered in an airtight container in the refrigerator for 2 days before cooking; it isn't mandatory, but it will help boost the flavor.

Transfer to a medium saucepan. Whisk the agar powder into the liquid. Heat on medium-high, lower the heat to medium and cook for 7 minutes to fully activate the agar, lowering the heat if needed once the mixture thickens to avoid scorching. Be sure to whisk constantly. The mixture will be quite thick but still pourable.

Equally divide the mixture among the prepared ramekins, and use a rubber spatula to spread the tops evenly. Let cool to room temperature, then transfer into the refrigerator to set. Once completely cooled and firmed up (at least 2 hours), remove the cheeses from the ramekins by shaking gently to coax them out.

Store covered in the refrigerator for at least 5 days. The longer the better to let the flavors develop and ripen. Use within 2 weeks.

When ready to use, place the spice mixture of choice in a shallow pan. Gently roll the cheese wheels in the spices and shake the excess off. Serve with crackers or crusty bread.

Chapter Three

SWEET

Time for dessert: the final frontier to any meal worth its weight in gold. While most of us are fond of simple things, such as vanilla ice cream and apple pie, there's more to sweet-toothed life than this. Throw some Miso Caramel (page 143) on that à la mode action, and now we're talking!

By expertly using ingredients, such as zingy citrus and pomegranate molasses, a fantastic depth of flavor can be added to your favorite food cravings. Not to mention what you can do when you daringly incorporate ingredients that are commonly considered to be more savory than sweet, such as tamari, sumac and yeast extract (for real).

You know how a pinch of salt brings out the sweetness and balances out your muffins, pies, lemon curd and other similar treats? That's the same concept here—only made more creative. Of course, it's not about dumping in a pound of sumac, adding the whole jar of Marmite or pouring in the bottle of tamari to show off what a daredevil you are. It's about using just enough to make you go "Oh, I get it. Now give me more!" So get ready to see how these individual ingredients take a more traditional dish to a whole new, bolder territory.

PEACHY TAMARI CREAMY FARINA

In A Hurry • Oil-Free

While I usually lean more towards crunchy cold cereal rather than porridge-like hot cereal, I make an exception for this recipe. It's all about the caramelized, subtly tamari-flavored peaches here, with the added crunch of the almonds and the spiciness of the optional crystallized ginger. Note that if you don't have a grill, preparing the peaches in a large skillet will do the trick too. You're looking for a caramelized outside, but the peaches must remain firm.

YIELD: 2 servings

---

2 large, firm peaches

¼ cup (80 g) naturally sweetened apricot jam

Juice from 1 large lemon (about 3 tbsp [45 ml])

2½ tsp (13 ml) reduced-sodium tamari

1½ cups (355 ml) unsweetened vanilla or plain plant-based milk

⅓ cup (55 g) uncooked brown rice farina or whole-wheat farina

½ tsp pure vanilla extract

Dry roasted whole almonds, coarsely chopped

Crystallized ginger, coarsely chopped (optional)

Brown rice syrup or agave nectar, for serving

Heat a grill or large pan. Quarter the peaches, remove the pit. Halve each quarter. Set aside.

In a medium bowl, whisk to combine the jam, lemon juice and tamari. Brush the peaches with the mixture. Place the peaches on the grill, making sure not to discard the remaining jam mixture. Grill the peaches just to get slight grill marks, about 5 minutes total, flipping once halfway through. Remove them before they get mushy, even if there are no visible marks. Set aside. You can chop them when ready to eat. If the skin is thick, you can also elect to peel the peaches at this point.

Place the milk and farina in a medium pot. Cook on medium heat until the mixture is thickened and the farina is tender, about 8 minutes. Stir frequently with a wooden spoon. Stir the remaining jam mixture into the farina along with the vanilla.

Divide the farina between two bowls. Top with peaches, almonds and ginger (if using). Drizzle syrup to taste.

MANGO PAPAYA SMOOTHIE BOWL

Gluten-Free • In A Hurry • Oil-Free • Soy-Free

I'm entirely new to smoothie bowls, but I can see their appeal. Add-ins are the best part of ice cream so why not make smoothies a little more interesting, better-looking and possibly more filling too (depending on said toppings)?

Speaking of toppings, they are yours to pick. Just don't skip the beautiful golden syrup to add a little sweetness, tartness and flavor boost. You can replace the coconut milk with any unsweetened plain vegan yogurt you like. If the results are too thick for your taste, you can thin them out with an unsweetened plain plant-based milk of choice. I like using canned coconut milk because it gets super light and airy when blended with the fruit. If you want the resulting smoothie to be thicker, use frozen mango and papaya. Note that the recipe icons might not apply depending on the toppings you choose and if you make the aforementioned changes on the milk and yogurt front.

YIELD: 2 servings, 1/3 cup (80 ml) syrup

FOR THE SYRUP

1/4 cup (80 g) agave nectar

1 tbsp (15 ml) lemon juice

1/4 tsp ground ginger

1/4 tsp ground turmeric

FOR THE BOWLS

6 oz (170 g) mango flesh, chopped

6 oz (170 g) papaya flesh, chopped

1 frozen, peeled medium banana

1/2 cup (120 ml) unsweetened canned coconut milk or coconut cream

Juice from 1 lime (2 tbsp [30 ml])

Toppings: Super seed and sprouted grain blend, chia seeds, hemp seeds, granola, fresh fruit, toasted unsweetened coconut flakes, cacao nibs

To make the syrup, stir together the agave, lemon juice, ginger and turmeric in a small mason jar. Cover and let stand while preparing the bowls. The syrup can be stored in an airtight jar in the refrigerator for up to 2 weeks. Stir again before use.

To make the bowls, place the mango, papaya, banana, coconut milk and lime juice in a blender. Blend until perfectly smooth and combined. Transfer to two bowls. Drizzle with syrup to taste, and cover with your toppings of choice. Serve immediately.

MISO SWEET COOKIES

Who said miso can only be used in salty dishes? These cookies certainly didn't. They only keep getting better, too: eat one still warm from the oven or cooled the next day. But you might find them at their unbeatable best after a trip to the freezer, wrapped tightly and then (obviously) thawed. Pass the plant-based milk, as well as the self-control, please.

YIELD: 26 cookies

¾ cup (144 g) Sucanat

¾ cup (144 g) turbinado sugar

¼ cup (72 g) white miso

6 tbsp (90 ml) grapeseed oil or other neutral-flavored oil

2½ tsp (13 ml) pure vanilla extract

4 tsp (16 g) whole white chia seeds or ground flax seeds

¼ cup (60 ml) fresh orange juice

2 tsp (4 g) dried Valencia orange peel or zest from a fresh organic orange

2 cups (160 g) old-fashioned rolled oats

1½ cups (180 g) whole-wheat pastry flour or all-purpose flour

¾ tsp baking powder

Pinch coarse kosher salt (if you like salty, otherwise optional)

¼ cup (weight will vary, approximately 30 g) seeds, sprouted grains, chopped nuts of choice or a combination

¼ cup (30 g) unsweetened shredded coconut

Preheat the oven to 350°F (180°C, or gas mark 4). Line two cookie sheets with parchment paper or silicone baking mats.

In a large bowl, whisk to combine the sugars, miso, oil, vanilla, chia seeds, orange juice and orange peel. Add the oats, flour, baking powder, salt, seeds and coconut on top. Stir the ingredients to thoroughly combine. Use 2 packed tablespoons (40 g) of dough per cookie, placing 13 per sheet as they don't spread much while baking. Flatten almost to the desired shape, using the palm of your hand.

Bake for 16 to 18 minutes, or until golden brown around the edges. Leave on the sheets for 10 minutes before transferring to a cooling rack. These cookies are great eaten warm or cooled. Store in an airtight container for up to 3 days, or freeze tightly wrapped for up to 3 months.

POMEGRANATE SUMAC BERRIES

Gluten-Free • Oil-Free

Two of my most recently discovered ingredient BFFs are pomegranate molasses and ground sumac. They are extremely versatile and refreshing, and they turn the simplest dishes into a fancy, taste bud-tickling feast. Both have a pleasantly tart flavor, which pairs so well with the sweetness of berries. Sumac has a very subtle salty quality to it, which also balances out the sweetness of this dish.

YIELD: 4 servings

1 pound (454 g) medium-sized fresh strawberries, hulled and halved

2 tbsp (30 ml) Pomegranate Molasses (page 186)

1/2 tsp ground sumac

6 oz (170 g) fresh raspberries

8 scoops vegan vanilla ice cream (slightly softened) or yogurt

1/2 cup (85 g) pomegranate arils (seeds)

Chopped raw or roasted pistachios

Preheat the oven to 375°F (190°C, or gas mark 5). Place the strawberries in an 8-inch (20-cm) square baking pan. Drizzle the molasses, sprinkle the sumac on top and gently fold to combine.

Bake until the strawberries soften and the molasses thickens slightly, about 20 minutes, gently folding occasionally. Set aside and let it cool to room temperature. Gently fold the raspberries into the strawberries.

To serve, divide the berries among four bowls. Top with two scoops of ice cream, pomegranate arils and chopped pistachios. The meltier the ice cream, the tastier the dessert.

TRIPLE C TRUFFLES

Gluten-Free • Oil-Free

Truffles used to be among my favorite chocolates to enjoy as an omnivore, so I just had to include a recipe in this book. I made mine spicy, using chipotle powder that doesn't overpower the chocolate, rather making its presence noticed as a pleasant, very quiet after-burn. Since ingredients do vary, I suggest making it once as listed, then playing around with the amount of spices in future batches to suit your own personal taste. If you don't care for darker, ever-so-slightly bitter types of chocolate, you can use a combination of dark and semisweet, or use only semisweet for (surprise, surprise) sweeter results.

YIELD: 8 large or 16 small truffles

$3\frac{1}{2}$ oz (100 g) vegan dark chocolate, chopped

2 tbsp–$\frac{1}{4}$ cup (30-60 ml) coconut cream (Use the lower amount if the cream is thin. Use the larger amount if it is really thick.)

2 tsp (13 g) pure maple syrup or agave nectar

$\frac{1}{8}$ tsp instant coffee powder

$\frac{1}{16}$ tsp chipotle powder

$\frac{1}{8}$ tsp ground cinnamon

Pinch coarse kosher salt

$\frac{1}{8}$ tsp pure vanilla extract

2 tbsp (18 g) cacao nibs, crushed into coarse powder, more if needed

2 tbsp (14 g) pistachio meal, more if needed

Line a plate with parchment paper or wax paper. Place the chocolate in a medium, heat-proof bowl.

Whisk to combine the cream, syrup, coffee powder, chipotle powder, cinnamon and salt in a small saucepan. Heat on medium to dissolve the coffee powder and until heated through, about 2 minutes. Remove from the heat and combine with the vanilla. Pour onto the chocolate and stir to melt. Leave at room temperature to thicken slightly, for 45 minutes.

Scoop 1 tablespoon (20 g) of the soft mixture for larger truffles, or $1\frac{1}{2}$ teaspoons (10 g) for smaller truffles, and spoon out onto the paper. Repeat with the remaining mixture. You should get 8 large or 16 small truffles in all, but the yield might vary slightly.

Refrigerate until firm, about 10 to 30 minutes depending on temperature. Shape the mixture into round truffles, and coat half of the truffles by rolling into ground cacao nibs and the rest with pistachio meal, using a fork if needed. Store in the refrigerator for up to 4 days, but be sure to serve at room temperature for the ultimate creaminess and flavor.

GRILLED PINEAPPLE WITH TAHINI LIME NUTS

Gluten-Free • Soy-Free

Watch out for those nuts: Resist snacking on too many of them before eating a bowl of this dessert, or you're bound to run out. Not that I speak from experience or anything. Besides, you're going to love how the caramelized parts of the richly flavored pineapple pair so well with the buttery, zesty nuts!

Choose the combination of unsalted dry roasted nuts you prefer, just as long as they are of similar size for even cooking.

YIELD: 8 servings, 2 cups (240 g) nuts, 2 cups (320 g) crema

FOR THE GLAZED NUTS

$1/2$ cup (60 g) unsalted dry roasted pistachios

$1/2$ cup (60 g) unsalted dry roasted cashew pieces

$1/3$ cup (56 g) unsalted dry roasted peanuts

2 tbsp (30 ml) lime juice

2 tbsp (40 g) pure maple syrup or agave nectar

1 tbsp (16 g) tahini paste

1 tbsp (12 g) coconut sugar or evaporated cane juice

Pinch coarse kosher salt

Pinch cayenne pepper (optional), plus extra for serving

$1/32$ tsp baking soda

$1/4$ tsp pure vanilla extract

FOR THE COCONUT CREMA

Chilled unsweetened coconut cream scooped from 1 (14-oz [414-ml]) refrigerated can

1 tbsp (15 ml) pure maple syrup

Zest of half a lime

FOR THE PINEAPPLE

1 fresh, ripe pineapple, rind removed, cored or not, cut into $1/2$-inch (1.3-cm) slices

2 tbsp (30 ml) lime juice

1 tbsp (15 ml) pure maple syrup

1 tbsp (15 ml) melted coconut oil

(continued)

GRILLED PINEAPPLE WITH TAHINI LIME NUTS (CONT.)

To make the nuts, combine the pistachios, cashews and peanuts in a heat-proof medium bowl. Whisk to combine the lime juice, syrup, tahini, sugar, salt and cayenne (if using) in a small saucepan. Heat on medium heat and cook for 5 minutes, whisking occasionally and adjusting the heat as needed to prevent scorching. Remove from the heat and whisk in the baking soda. The mixture will foam slightly. Add the vanilla and whisk to combine. Pour onto the nuts and stir to thoroughly combine.

Preheat the oven to 300°F (150°C, or gas mark 2). Place the nuts evenly on a large rimmed baking sheet lined with parchment paper. Bake for 6 minutes. Let cool and coarsely chop.

To make the crema, place the coconut cream, syrup and lime zest in a chilled medium bowl. Beat with a hand mixer until the crema doubles in volume, about 5 minutes. Cover and chill until ready to serve.

To make the pineapple, whisk to combine the lime juice, syrup and oil in a medium-sized bowl. Coat the pineapple slices with the mixture. Sear the pineapple rings on a heated grill until marks appear, about 5 minutes on each side. Let stand 10 minutes. Serve as is or chopped with a few spoonfuls of crema and chopped nuts.

BALSAMIC BERRY PANNA COTTA

Gluten-Free

Panna cotta means cooked cream in Italian. The vinegar reduction used here brings a zingy, refined punch to the berries, and it pairs extremely well with the creamy taste of the strawberry panna cotta. Just be sure not to cook the reduction on too high a temperature, otherwise it will taste bitter and remain vinegary.

I have quite a few acquaintances who are allergic to nuts, so for equality's sake I used tofu here instead of the cashew cream the vegan world loves so much. If you would rather go with cashews, soak the raw cashews in a generous amount of filtered water overnight. Drain and rinse them, and blend them with just enough water to get to the texture of firm silken tofu. You will need approximately 1 cup (120 g) of raw cashews to yield 8 ounces (227 g) of cashew cream to replace the tofu in this recipe.

YIELD: 8 desserts (will vary depending on mold)

FOR THE BERRIES

1/2 cup (120 ml) white balsamic vinegar

2 tsp (13 g) agave nectar

1/2 tsp pure vanilla extract

Generous 1/2 cup (90 g) fresh blackberries, gently washed and thoroughly drained

Generous 1/2 cup (90 g) fresh blueberries, gently washed and thoroughly drained

FOR THE PANNA COTTA

1 cup (195 g) gently packed and slightly heaping chopped fresh strawberries

1 tbsp (12 g) evaporated cane juice

1/4 cup (80 g) agave nectar

1 tsp (5 ml) pure vanilla extract

Pinch coarse kosher salt

Oil, for molds

3/4 cup (180 ml) unsweetened canned coconut cream

8 oz (227 g) silken tofu

1 tbsp (15 ml) lemon juice

1 tsp (3 g) agar powder

Dried culinary rose petals, for garnish (optional)

(continued)

BALSAMIC BERRY PANNA COTTA (CONT.)

To make the berries, place the vinegar and agave in a small saucepan. Bring to a low boil, reduce the heat and simmer until reduced to about 3 tablespoons (45 ml). You can eyeball this; the reduction should be thickened and light golden. Be sure to stir frequently while simmering. Reducing the vinegar will take approximately 8 to 10 minutes. Remove from the heat and add the vanilla. Set aside to cool. Once cooled, and only 30 minutes before serving the dessert, gently fold the berries into the syrup.

To make the panna cotta, place the berries and cane juice in a medium-sized, heat-proof glass bowl. Gently fold, cover and leave at room temperature for 30 minutes. Combine in a small blender with the agave, vanilla and salt. Blend until smooth. Strain through a fine-mesh sieve to remove the seeds. Transfer back to the medium bowl.

Very lightly brush eight $3^1/_4$ x $1^1/_4$-inch (8.3 x 3.2-cm) mini brioche molds (or any mold of similar size) with oil. Set aside.

Place the coconut cream, tofu and lemon juice in a blender. Blend until smooth. Transfer to a small saucepan. Whisk the agar into the mixture. Bring to a low boil, reduce the heat to low and cook for 5 minutes to activate the agar. Pour this mixture on top of the strawberry mixture, and whisk to thoroughly combine. Divide among the prepared molds. Let cool to room temperature before transferring to the refrigerator to firm for at least 3 hours. Remove the panna cotta from the molds by shaking gently to coax them out. If they resist, use a toothpick to help release them. Serve with the berries, and add rose petals as decoration if desired.

MISO CARAMEL

Gluten-Free • Oil-Free

This is a must-have on the Miso Caramel Galette (page 144). I find this thick yet pourable, pleasantly salty-sweet caramel is even more awesome when prepared with Sucanat (Sugar Cane Natural) than with light brown sugar. Who would have thought?

YIELD: About ¾ cup (200 g) caramel

---

2 tbsp (36 g) white miso

1 tsp (5 ml) pure vanilla extract

¾ cup plus 2 tbsp (165 g) Sucanat or ¾ cup (165 g) packed organic light brown sugar

¾ cup (180 ml) unsweetened canned coconut milk or coconut cream

In a small bowl, stir to combine the miso and vanilla. Set aside.

In a small saucepan, bring the Sucanat and milk to a boil on medium-high heat, stirring to dissolve the sugar crystals, about 1 minute. Continue to cook on medium heat, using a pastry brush to brush any sugar crystals from the sides of the saucepan. Do not stir at this point as this would cause crystallization. Cook until the bubbling mixture reaches 230°F (110°C) on a candy thermometer, adjusting the heat as needed. This will take about 8 minutes.

Turn off the heat, leaving the saucepan on the burner. Whisk the miso and vanilla preparation into the mixture. The miso might have trouble getting non-clumpy at first, but it will dissolve completely as the caramel is whisked while cooling down. Let it cool completely, whisking occasionally. Refrigerate in an airtight container for at least 1 hour or overnight. The caramel will thicken as it cools. This caramel can be drizzled on apple pie (page 124) and ice cream, or apple slices for dipping.

MISO CARAMEL GALETTE

A very flaky crust, salty-sweet caramel and tender apples make this galette my new favorite dessert. I bet you'll love it too! I found super sweet apples at the market and topped the pie with vegan vanilla ice cream, so extra sweetness wasn't needed. But if your apples aren't exceptionally sweet, and even more so if you don't plan on serving the galette with ice cream, consider tossing the apples with the optional 2 tablespoons (24 g) of light brown sugar and spices.

YIELD: 4 servings

1¼ cups (150 g) whole-wheat pastry flour, all-purpose flour or light spelt flour

2 tbsp plus 2 tsp (32 g) organic light brown sugar, divided

¼ tsp fine sea salt or ½ tsp coarse kosher salt

Scant ¼ cup (55 ml) grapeseed oil or olive oil

2 tsp (10 ml) apple cider vinegar

Ice cold water, as needed

Almond meal, to lightly cover bottom

5 small apples (14 oz [397 g]), peeled if desired, cored and cut into 2 slices each

½ tsp ground ginger (optional)

½ tsp ground cinnamon (optional)

2 tbsp (30 g) Miso Caramel (page 143), plus extra for serving

Preheat the oven to 375°F (190°C, or gas mark 5). Line a large rimmed baking sheet with parchment paper. In a large bowl, use a fork to combine the flour, 2 teaspoons (8 g) of sugar and salt. Drizzle the oil and vinegar on top, and use the fork to create crumbles. Add water as needed, stirring with the fork until a dough forms; it should be neither too wet, nor too dry. I usually need about ¼ cup (60 ml) water, added 1 tablespoon (15 ml) at a time. Shape into a ball and flatten into a disk.

To roll out the dough, you can either use the parchment paper mentioned above or a silicone baking mat that you will use to flip the dough onto the paper-lined baking sheet. I find the silicone baking mat adheres better to the counter while working. Using a rolling pin, roll out the dough into an approximately 10-inch (25-cm) circle. Transfer the dough by carefully flipping the silicone baking mat on top of the prepared sheet.

Evenly sprinkle a handful of almond meal in the center, leaving about 1½ inches (3.8 cm) from the edge. In a large bowl, toss the apples with the remaining 2 tablespoons (24 g) of sugar and the ginger and cinnamon (if using). Arrange the apple slices in the crust, overlapping slightly, and cover the area that has almond meal on it. Drizzle 2 tablespoons (30 g) of caramel evenly on top. Fold the edges on top of the fruit, overlapping where needed and pressing slightly to seal. Bake for 50 minutes or until golden brown. The apples should be tender. Place on a wire rack to cool before slicing.

Serve with vegan ice cream or whipped coconut cream—and extra caramel, of course.

*See photo on page 124.

ORANGE CREAMSICLE TARTLETS WITH GINGER PEARS

Because no one can say no to a fancy and slightly tart tartlet!

YIELD: 6 tartlets

FOR THE SYRUP PEARS

2 small Asian pears (about 100 g each), quartered, cored and thinly sliced

3 tbsp (45 ml) lemon juice

Scant 1/2 cup (105 ml) water

Scant 1/4 cup (40 g) evaporated cane juice or organic granulated sugar

Generous 1/2 tsp ground ginger or 1 tsp (2 g) grated fresh ginger root

Pinch coarse kosher salt

FOR THE CRUST

Nonstick cooking spray or oil spray

3/4 cup (90 g) whole-wheat pastry or all-purpose flour

Pinch coarse kosher salt

1/4 tsp ground ginger

2 tbsp (30 ml) grapeseed or light olive oil

2 tbsp (40 g) agave nectar

2 tsp (10 ml) water

FOR THE ORANGE CREAM FILLING

Scant 1 cup (205 g) Simplest Nut-Free Cream (page 168)

1 organic orange, zested and juiced (use 1/2 cup [120 ml] juice)

1/4 cup (80 g) agave nectar

Pinch kosher salt

1 tbsp (8 g) organic cornstarch

1/2 tsp agar powder

1 tsp (5 ml) pure vanilla extract

More organic orange zest, for garnish

To make the pears, place the pears in a medium-sized, heat-resistant bowl. Add the lemon juice and fold to combine. The lemon juice will prevent browning. In a small saucepan, combine the water, cane juice, ginger and salt. Bring to a low boil on medium-high heat, lower the heat to a simmer and simmer for 4 minutes. Let cool for 5 minutes before pouring on top of the pears. Cover with a plate and set aside until ready to use. The pears can be stored in an airtight container in the refrigerator for up to 3 days if prepared ahead.

(continued)

ORANGE CREAMSICLE TARTLETS WITH GINGER PEARS (CONT.)

To make the crust, preheat the oven to 325°F (170°C, or gas mark 3). Lightly coat 6 (3-inch [8-cm]) mini tart pans with spray. In a bowl, use a fork to combine the flour, salt and ginger. Pour the oil and agave on top, stir with a fork to mix. Add the water as needed to obtain a dough that is neither too wet nor too dry. Divide the dough among the prepared pans, about 1 slightly heaping, packed tablespoon (25 g) each. Press down evenly at the bottom and on the sides of the pan. Lightly prick the crust with the tines of a fork to prevent bubbling.

Place the pans close to the bottom burner of the oven because the top of the crusts will bake faster. Bake 14 to 16 minutes, or until golden brown all over. Keep an eye on the oven to prevent burning. Remove from the oven and place on a cooling rack. Once cool enough to handle, remove the crusts from the pans and let cool completely.

To make the filling, in a small saucepan, vigorously whisk to combine the cream, orange juice, agave, salt, cornstarch and agar. Be sure no clumps remain. Bring to a low boil on medium-high heat, lower the heat to a simmer and cook for 5 minutes to activate the agar. Be sure to whisk constantly. The mixture should reach the thickness of pudding after 5 minutes. If it doesn't, keep cooking until it does, still whisking constantly. Stir the vanilla and orange zest into the filling. Set aside to cool, whisking occasionally to prevent lumps.

To assemble, fill the cooled crusts with cooled cream filling. Use a spatula to flatten the filling in each crust. Loosely cover with plastic wrap. Chill for 1 hour. There might be leftovers, so just place them in a small bowl, cover with plastic wrap and enjoy them chilled.

When ready to serve, top each tartlet with a few slices of pears. Be sure not to add too much of the ginger syrup so that the tartlets don't get soggy, and add extra orange zest on top. The tartlets are best eaten the day they are prepared.

POMEGRANATE STRAWBERRY GRANITA

Gluten-Free • Oil-Free • Soy-Free

The intense flavor popping out of this frozen looker makes for the perfect ending to any summer meal. Be sure to use the sweetest and ripest summer strawberries to make up for the tartness of the molasses!

YIELD: 4 servings

---

¹/₃ cup (80 ml) water

3 tbsp (36 g) organic evaporated cane juice or granulated sugar

¹/₂ tsp ground ginger

Slightly heaping 2³/₄ cups (400 g) fresh strawberries, hulled and halved, divided

¹/₄ cup plus 1 tbsp (75 ml) Pomegranate Molasses (page 186), divided

¹/₂ tsp pure vanilla extract

Make a simple syrup by combining the water, sugar and ginger in a small saucepan. Bring to a low boil, lower the heat and simmer until the sugar crystals are dissolved, stirring frequently, about 2 minutes. Remove from the heat and let cool to room temperature.

Blend the syrup with a heaping 2 cups (300 g) of the strawberries, ¹/₄ cup (60 ml) of pomegranate molasses and the vanilla, until smooth. Pass through a fine-mesh sieve to remove the seeds, and transfer to an 8-inch (20-cm) glass baking dish.

Place in the freezer for 1 hour. Stir the mixture and scrape the sides to prevent ice crystals from forming, creating flakes. Repeat the process every 30 minutes for a total of 4 hours.

About 30 minutes before serving, chop the remaining ²/₃ cup (100 g) of strawberry halves and combine them with 1 tablespoon (15 ml) of pomegranate molasses. Serve the granita in small glass bowls, and spoon the strawberries on top.

TUNISIAN BAHARAT ROASTED PLUOTS

Gluten-Free • Soy-Free

Who would have thought savory ingredients in sweet desserts would be so fantastic? My favorite part here is the tingle left on the tongue by the pepper from the baharat mix. It's not overly peppery at all, but subtle and unexpected enough to be highly enjoyable. And it makes for a rather fancy dessert, despite its simplicity.

YIELD: 4 servings

---

³/₄ cup (180 g) solid coconut cream scooped from the top of a chilled can of coconut milk

¹/₄ tsp pure vanilla extract

A few drops culinary rose water (optional)

2 tsp (10 ml) roasted walnut oil or melted coconut oil

4 medium to large firm fresh pluots, red plums or black plums, halved and pitted

¹/₄ cup (80 g) brown rice syrup

2 tbsp (30 ml) lemon juice

2 tbsp (30 ml) fresh orange juice

Generous ¹/₄ tsp Tunisian Baharat (page 162)

A few crumbled culinary rose petals and crushed pink peppercorn, for garnish (optional)

Place the coconut cream in a chilled bowl, along with the vanilla and rose water (if using). Using a hand mixer fitted with a whisk attachment, whisk the cream until it is fluffy and firm, about 5 minutes. Cover and refrigerate for at least 2 hours before use.

Preheat the oven to 375°F (190°C, or gas mark 5). Brush the oil on the bottom of an 8-inch (20-cm) square baking dish. Place the halved pluots cut-side up in the dish.

In a small bowl, whisk to combine the syrup, lemon juice, orange juice and baharat. Pour onto the pluots, then flip them cut-side down in the dish.

Bake for 10 minutes, then flip and bake another 5 to 10 minutes until tender but not mushy. If the fruit is soft and ready sooner than the syrup has time to thicken, gently take the pluots out and set them aside on a plate, pour the syrup into a small saucepan, and reduce it to half over low heat at a slow boil until it is thicker about 5 minutes. It will continue to thicken as it cools. Let cool slightly before serving with coconut cream and garnishes of choice.

MARMITE PEANUT HALVA

Oil-Free • Soy-Free

This halva is sweet and at the same time just a little savory. The recipe makes for a small batch. Once you're familiar with it, you can easily double it—if you have enough self-control to not eat the whole thing on your own. You can also adapt it to your liking by using different kinds of nut or seed butters and other nuts or seeds as well.

Start small with the amount of yeast spread if you're new to it, and adjust the quantity in future batches. Keep in mind that some yeast spreads are stronger-tasting than others. We're looking at you, Vegemite. Ideally, go with unsalted peanut butter as the yeast spread will obviously bring its own saltiness. If you cannot find unsalted peanut butter, definitely go with the lower amount of yeast spread.

YIELD: 16 (1-inch [2.5-cm]) squares

½ cup (110 g) packed organic light brown sugar or Sucanat

6 tbsp (90 ml) unsweetened canned coconut cream

1 to 2 tsp (8 to 16 g) yeast spread (such as Marmite, Vegemite or Cenovis), to taste

1 tsp (5 ml) pure vanilla extract

½ cup (128 g) natural crunchy peanut butter (preferably unsalted)

¼ cup (30 g) unsalted dry roasted peanuts

Be sure to have all the ingredients measured and ready on the counter before getting started. Place the sugar and coconut cream in a medium saucepan. Bring to a boil on medium-high heat, stirring to dissolve the sugar crystals. Continue to cook on medium heat, using a pastry brush to brush any sugar crystals from the sides of the saucepan. Do not stir.

Cook until the bubbling mixture reaches 240°F (115°C) on a candy thermometer. This will take about 8 to 10 minutes. Turn off the heat. Use a whisk to stir in the yeast spread to ensure that it gets fully dissolved. Then stir in the vanilla, followed by the peanut butter. Make sure each ingredient is fully incorporated. Fold the peanuts into the mixture with a rubber spatula.

Transfer the mixture to a small baking sheet lined with parchment paper, and evenly spread it into a 4-inch (10-cm) square. Let cool completely before transferring to the refrigerator to further set for at least 2 hours or, even better, overnight. Cut into small portions, and enjoy with a hot cup of tea or coffee. Leftovers can be stored in the refrigerator, wrapped tightly, for up to 2 weeks.

Chapter Four

STAPLES

All cupboards, refrigerators and freezers need a few good staples, always at the ready whenever you crave meals bursting with big flavors. That's where this staple-centric chapter comes in with its offerings of striking spice mixes, umami-packed broth, bright and tangy finishing sauces and more.

These recipes are included for anyone who has trouble finding some of their store-bought counterparts locally and for those of us who prefer to make everything from scratch. Most of these staples can or must be prepared ahead of time so that the total cooking time for the recipes in which they make an appearance is reasonable. I like to dedicate a couple of hours during the weekend to rebuild my collection of such staples. Then I store them neatly and clearly labeled so that I can remember what's what.

EASY AS 2, 2, 2 BROTH MIX

Gluten-Free • In A Hurry • Oil-Free • Soy-Free

This broth mix is as quick and easy as 1, 2, 3. You probably won't even need the actual recipe after making it once, because the quantity of almost every ingredient is identical: two teaspoons of each, except for the nutritional yeast. Woo! Adapt it to your own taste and according to what's available in your pantry. Both the tomato powder and mushroom powder are optional, but I highly recommend them to get that umami boost.

To make broth out of this mix, use 1 teaspoon (2 g) for every cup (235 ml) of water for a mellow broth. Use 1 tablespoon (6 g) for every cup (235 ml) of water for a flavor-packed broth.

YIELD: 1¼ cups (113 g)

---

1 cup (80 g) nutritional yeast

2 tsp (3 g) onion powder

2 tsp (2 g) garlic powder

2 tsp (12 g) fine regular or smoked sea salt, or a combination of both

2 tsp (4 g) sweet or smoked paprika, or a combination of both

2 tsp (2 g) Italian seasoning or other mix of dried herbs of choice

2 tsp (10 g) dried tomato powder (optional)

2 tsp (3 g) dried shiitake powder or porcini powder (optional)

Ground rainbow or other peppercorn, to taste

Place the nutritional yeast, onion powder, garlic powder, salt, paprika, Italian seasoning, tomato powder (if using), shiitake powder (if using) and peppercorn in a large mason jar. Screw the lid on tightly, and shake to thoroughly combine. Store at room temperature or in the refrigerator for up to 1 month.

HASH SPICE

Gluten-Free • In A Hurry • Oil-Free • Soy-Free

Sprinkle this flavor-boosting spice mix on top of tacos (page 101), Hash and Spice (page 83) or anywhere that calls for a dusting of savory goodness.

YIELD: Scant 1/2 cup (54 g)

---

3 tbsp (23 g) dry roasted unsalted almonds, pepitas or pine nuts, coarsely chopped

3 tbsp (15 g) nutritional yeast

1/2 tsp onion powder

1/2 tsp smoked paprika

1/2 tsp ancho chile powder

1/2 tsp ground cumin

1/2 tsp ground coriander

Generous 1/2 tsp smoked sea salt

Place the almonds, nutritional yeast, onion powder, paprika, ancho powder, cumin, coriander and salt in a mini food processor or coffee grinder. Grind until finely ground. Transfer to an airtight container. Store at room temperature for up to 1 week or in the refrigerator for up to 1 month.

*See photo on page 157.

RAS EL HANOUT

Gluten-Free • In A Hurry • Oil-Free • Soy-Free

Arabic for "top of the shop," *ras el hanout* is a rich and fragrant Moroccan spice blend. Its composition varies greatly, but a few typical spices are: coriander, cumin, cinnamon, nutmeg, peppercorn and paprika. Some blends can contain up to 100 spices! I kept things manageable here by using less and put it to great use in several recipes, such as Very Tahini Teffballs (page 81), Moroccan-Flavored Stuffed Squash (page 95) and more.

YIELD: Scant ¼ cup (23 g)

---

1 tbsp (6 g) ground cumin (from toasted seeds)

1 tbsp (6 g) ground coriander (from toasted seeds)

Few turns white peppercorn grinder (optional)

½ tsp ground cinnamon

½ tsp ground allspice

½ tsp sweet paprika

¼ tsp ground ginger

⅛ tsp ground nutmeg

⅛ tsp ground turmeric

Whisk the cumin, coriander, peppercorn (if using), cinnamon, allspice, paprika, ginger, nutmeg and turmeric in a small bowl. Transfer to an airtight container and store at room temperature for up to 1 month. The fresher the better, so keep your yield small.

*See photo on page 163.

SHICHIMI TOGARASHI

Gluten-Free • In A Hurry • Oil-Free • Soy-Free

In Japanese, *shichimi* means seven and *togarashi* means chile. Thus, this Japanese spice mixture contains seven ingredients. Try it on Chazuke (page 33), Asian-Inspired Fondue (page 19), Well-Dressed Cashew Wheels (page 123) or even simply sprinkled on ever-popular avocado toast and you'll see why it has become a must-have in my pantry.

YIELD: ¼ cup (32 g)

---

2 tsp (4 g) red or green Szechuan peppercorn (substitute white peppercorn if Szechuan is unavailable)

2 tsp (2 g) finely ground roasted nori sheet

2 tsp (4 g) dried Valencia orange peel

2 tsp (4 g) Aleppo pepper flakes or other red pepper flakes, or to taste

2 tsp (5 g) roasted black sesame seeds

2 tsp (5 g) roasted white sesame seeds, hemp seeds or poppy seeds

½ tsp garlic powder

Use a mortar and pestle to crush or grind the peppercorn. Add the nori, orange peel, pepper flakes, black and white sesame seeds and garlic powder to the mortar and pestle. Stir to combine, crushing slightly to extract flavors.

Alternatively, use a small food processor to grind the peppercorn. Add the rest of the ingredients and pulse twice to combine. Store in an airtight container at room temperature for up to 2 weeks.

CHINESE FIVE-SPICE POWDER

Gluten-Free • In A Hurry • Oil-Free • Soy-Free

This one is quick and flavorful. If Szechuan peppercorn is hard to locate, use the same quantity of white peppercorn (or half if it's particularly strong).

YIELD: 2 tablespoons (16 g)

2 tsp (4 g) green or red Szechuan peppercorn

2 tsp (4 g) fennel seeds

2 whole star anise

1 tiny cinnamon stick (about 0.1 oz [3 g]), broken into smaller pieces

1/2–3/4 tsp ground cloves, to taste

Toast the peppercorn, fennel seeds and star anise in a small saucepan on low heat just until they become fragrant, about 2 minutes. Be sure to stir often to prevent burning. Transfer to a small food processor along with the cinnamon stick and cloves, and blend until finely ground. Store in an airtight container at room temperature for up to 2 weeks. The fresher the better, so keep your batches small unless you use the mix quite frequently.

TUNISIAN BAHARAT

Gluten-Free • In A Hurry • Oil-Free • Soy-Free

Let this spice mix tingle your tongue in Tunisian Baharat Roasted Pluots (page 150), Harira (page 102) or even on top of your morning oatmeal to kick your taste buds awake.

YIELD: 1 1/2 teaspoons (6 g)

1 tsp (2 g) whole rainbow peppercorn

1 tiny cinnamon stick (about 0.1 oz [3 g]), broken into smaller pieces

1 tsp (0.3 g) culinary rose leaves

Place the peppercorn, cinnamon and rose leaves in a spice grinder, and grind into a fine powder. Store in an airtight container at room temperature for up to 1 month.

HARISSA PASTE

Gluten-Free • Soy-Free

A frequent flier in North African and Middle Eastern cuisines, harissa paste is a fiery condiment that is even greater homemade. If you are a little pressed for time, consider making Harissa Dry Mix (page 166) instead. I always have both handy and can't pick a favorite!

Here, both the paste and dry mix yield the most amazing results, especially compared to store-bought. So pick either form of harissa according to your preference and needs. Try using it in Tahini Harissa Toast (page 109), Harira (page 102) and more.

YIELD: Scant 1 cup (230 g) paste

1 oz (28 g) dried guajillo chile pods, cored, seeded and rinsed

1 oz (28 g) dried árbol chile pods, cored, seeded and rinsed

2 cups (470 ml) hot water

1 tsp (2 g) caraway seeds

1 tsp (2 g) coriander seeds

1 tsp (2 g) cumin seeds

1 tsp (2 g) smoked paprika

1 tsp (2 g) Aleppo pepper flakes

1 tsp (2 g) ancho chile powder

1 tsp (2 g) chipotle powder

1/2 tsp coarse kosher salt

2 tsp (11 g) double-concentrated tomato paste

1 tbsp (15 ml) roasted hazelnut or pistachio oil

1 large clove garlic, grated

Place the peppers in a heat-proof bowl and add hot water on top. Soak until softened, about 40 minutes. Drain but reserve the soaking liquid for other uses, storing in an airtight jar in the refrigerator for up to 1 week.

Lightly toast the caraway, coriander and cumin seeds in a skillet on low heat until fragrant, about 2 minutes, stirring frequently to prevent burning. Transfer to a spice grinder and grind into a fine powder. Transfer the peppers and powder to a food processor along with the paprika, pepper flakes, chile powders, salt, tomato paste, hazelnut oil and garlic. Process until smooth, stopping occasionally to scrape the sides of the machine with a rubber spatula. Add the chile water as needed to help the process along. You might need approximately 1/4 cup (60 ml).

Transfer to an airtight container, and top with just a drizzle of oil to keep the harissa fresh and moist. Store in the refrigerator for up to 2 weeks and cover with a little oil after each use.

HARISSA DRY MIX

Gluten-Free • In A Hurry • Oil-Free • Soy-Free

This powdered alternative to Harissa Paste (page 165) is perfect as an addition to spice mixes, on top of popcorn or anytime you run out of fresh paste and have a craving for smoky, spicy stuff! Try it in Harissa Citurs Veggies (page 115), Dukkah (page 55) and more.

YIELD: ¼ cup (34 g) dry mix

---

2 tsp (4 g) coriander seeds

2 tsp (4 g) cumin seeds

1 tsp (2 g) caraway seeds

¼ oz (7 g) dried guajillo chile pods, cored and seeded

¼ oz (7 g) dried árbol chile pods, cored and seeded

1 tsp (2 g) smoked paprika

1 tsp (2 g) Aleppo pepper flakes

½ tsp coarse kosher salt

½ tsp garlic powder

Lightly toast the coriander, cumin and caraway seeds in a skillet on low heat until fragrant, about 2 minutes, stirring frequently to prevent burning. Transfer to a spice grinder and grind into a fine powder.

Lightly toast the guajillo and árbol chiles in a skillet on low heat until fragrant, about 2 minutes, stirring frequently to prevent burning. Transfer them to the spice grinder and grind into a fine powder. Add the paprika, pepper flakes, salt and garlic powder, and grind to combine. Transfer to an airtight container and store at room temperature for up to 1 month. Remember: The fresher the better, so don't wait too long before using spices.

*See photo on page 164.

FABA-LOUS MAYO

Gluten-Free • Soy-Free

Aquafaba, also known as chickpea brine, is the liquid obtained from cooking chickpeas. Joël Roessel is the French chef who first noticed it could be turned into a foam and used in desserts. Goose Wohlt found out it could mimic egg whites, with astonishing results, in applications such as the one below. I love this mayo so much.

Yes, the amount of oil is nothing to sneeze at, but that is the case for all types of mayonnaise. The quantity of salt needed will depend upon how salty the aquafaba is. Start small with $^1/_4$ teaspoon, have a taste and increase the amount even after the mayo is emulsified; it won't harm it.

Don't use extra-virgin olive oil here. I love EVOO as much as the next person, but it will yield bitter results in this application and, by gum, what a waste that would be.

YIELD: $^3/_4$ to 1 cup (168 to 228 g)

FOR THE REGULAR VERSION
5 tbsp (75 ml) aquafaba (liquid from a can of chickpeas)

1 tsp (5 ml) lemon juice

1 tsp (5 g) mild Dijon mustard

1 tsp (5 ml) white balsamic vinegar

1 tsp (7 g) agave nectar

$^1/_4$ tsp coarse kosher salt, or to taste

$^1/_4$ tsp ground white peppercorn, or to taste (optional)

$^3/_4$ cup (180 ml) grapeseed oil or canola oil, up to $^1/_4$ cup (60 ml) more if needed

FOR THE CHIPOTLE VERSION
$1^1/_2$ tsp (7 g) tomato paste

$^3/_8$ tsp chipotle powder

$^1/_2$ tsp sweet paprika

$^1/_8$ tsp onion powder

$^1/_8$ tsp ground cumin

$^1/_{16}$ tsp garlic powder

FOR THE BASIL VERSION
$^1/_4$ cup (8 g) packed basil leaves, cut into chiffonade

1 clove garlic, grated

(continued)

FABA-LOUS MAYO (CONT.)

For best results, use aquafaba that is rather thick in order to obtain a thick mayonnaise.

Place the aquafaba, lemon juice, mustard, vinegar, agave, salt and pepper (if using) in a measuring cup fit for an immersion blender. Be sure to choose a cup that is large enough as the mayo volume will increase. Blend until combined and slightly thickened, about 2 minutes.

Very slowly drizzle the oil into the aquafaba mixture, blending continuously on high speed. The incorporation and emulsion of the oil should last approximately 4 minutes for a thick mayo-like result. If the results are still pourable and more dressing-like, slowly drizzle in up to an extra 1/4 cup (60 ml) of oil to help with the thickening.

To make either variation: Pick a version and add the ingredients after thickening the mayo. Blend until just incorporated. Cover and refrigerate for up to 1 week.

SIMPLEST NUT-FREE CREAM

Gluten-Free • In A Hurry • Oil-Free

Cashew creams are all the rage these days, and I've made and loved my own versions over the last few years. However, a few of my friends have family members who are allergic to nuts, so I wanted to offer an option for anyone who cannot enjoy nut-based creams. If you avoid soy, soak raw cashews in a generous amount of filtered water overnight. Drain and rinse them, and blend them with just enough water to get to the texture of firm silken tofu. You will need approximately 1 cup (120 g) of raw cashews to yield 8 ounces (227 g) of cashew cream to replace the tofu in this recipe.

YIELD: 1³/₄ cups (410 g)

3/4 cup (180 ml) unsweetened canned coconut cream

8 oz (227 g) extra-firm silken tofu

1 tbsp (15 ml) lemon juice

Pinch coarse kosher salt

Using a blender, blend the coconut cream, tofu, lemon juice and salt until perfectly smooth. Cover and refrigerate for at least 2 hours before serving. This cream will keep for up to 1 week.

*See photo on page 173.

SERUNDENG (INDONESIAN SEASONED COCONUT MIX)

Gluten-Free • In A Hurry • Soy-Free

Sprinkle this heavenly Indonesian seasoning mix on rice or noodle bowls, Indonesian-Inspired Rice Pancakes (page 105) and Quick and Easy Pad Thai (page 37). Caution: You might have a hard time not using it on everything.

Amchur powder is made from dried green mango. It can be found in the international section of well-stocked grocery stores.

YIELD: 1¼ cups (165 g)

½ cup (40 g) unsweetened, coarsely ground, shredded dried coconut

½ cup (70 g) dry roasted unsalted peanuts, coarsely chopped

⅓ cup (50 g) minced shallot or red onion

1½ tbsp (7 g) minced fresh lemongrass

1 clove garlic, grated

2 tbsp (24 g) coconut sugar or Sucanat

¾ tsp coarse kosher salt

1 tsp (2 g) ground coriander

½ tsp ground cumin

½ tsp ground ginger

⅛–¼ tsp cayenne pepper, to taste

1½ tsp (8 ml) melted coconut oil

⅛ tsp ground turmeric

⅛ tsp amchur powder, (optional)

Place the coconut, peanuts, shallot, lemongrass, garlic, coconut sugar, salt, coriander, cumin, ginger, cayenne and coconut oil in a large skillet. Toast on medium-high heat until dry, light golden brown and fragrant, about 8 minutes. Stir frequently and adjust the heat as needed to prevent burning.

Add the turmeric and amchur powder (if using), and toast for another 30 seconds. Remove from the heat and transfer evenly to a parchment paper to cool completely. The mixture will crisp up a bit as it cools. Store in an airtight container in the refrigerator or at room temperature for up to 1 week. Liberally sprinkle over vegetables, rice dishes, noodle dishes, curries and more.

CASHEW SPREAD

Gluten-Free • Oil-Free

Looking to put something a little more nutritious than vegan butter on your toast? Bored with vegan mayo in your sandwiches? Here's a great recipe for cashew spread that will also come in handy in the Piri Piri Pit-za (page 73) if store-bought vegan cream cheese isn't your cuppa.

YIELD: 1¼ cups (300 g)

---

1 cup (120 g) raw cashew pieces

Filtered water, to soak

¼ cup (60 g) plain unsweetened vegan yogurt (soy or coconut)

1 tbsp (15 ml) lemon juice

¼ tsp fine sea salt

Place the cashews in a medium-sized bowl. Cover with a generous amount of filtered water, about 1 inch (2.5 cm) above the cashews. Cover with plastic wrap and soak for 4 hours. Drain the cashews, and give them a quick rinse. Discard the soaking water. Transfer the cashews to a food processor or blender with the yogurt, lemon juice and salt. Process until completely smooth, adding filtered water if needed, 1 tablespoon (15 ml) at a time. Stop the machine occasionally to scrape the sides with a rubber spatula. Transfer the mixture into a medium-sized bowl and cover it with plastic wrap. Leave at room temperature for 24 hours or until the spread smells tangy. Refrigerate for up to 2 weeks.

FISH-FREE SAUCE

Gluten-Free • Oil-Free

If you're looking for the unmistakable umami boost from a sauce that elevates Asian-style dishes, here is a vegan option to keep little fishes happy and safe.

YIELD: ¾ cup (180 ml) sauce

1½ cups (355 ml) Mushroom Dashi (page 181) or water

2 tsp (3 g) dried shiitake powder

2 tsp (12 g) smoked sea salt

4 tsp (20 ml) reduced-sodium tamari

½ roasted nori sheet (0.14 oz [4 g])

Place the dashi, shiitake powder, salt, tamari and nori in a small saucepan. Bring to a boil, lower the heat and cook until reduced to about half the original amount, about 45 minutes. Adjust the heat as needed. Strain the nori and store the cooled fish-free sauce in an airtight container in the refrigerator for up to 2 weeks. Stir or shake before use, depending on the container used.

*See photo on page 174.

TERIYAKI SAUCE

Gluten-Free

This umami-rich, less-sweet-than-most teriyaki sauce belongs in tacos (page 23), bowls (page 46) and anywhere that calls for regular teriyaki sauce. If you cannot find dried shiitake powder, use Mushroom Dashi (page 181) instead of the water here.

YIELD: 1¼ cups (300 ml) sauce

---

1 tbsp (8 g) organic cornstarch

½ cup plus 2 tbsp (150 ml) water, divided

½ cup (120 ml) vegan mirin

½ cup (120 ml) reduced-sodium tamari

¼ cup (80 g) agave nectar

1 tsp (2 g) ground ginger

1 tsp (2 g) dried shiitake powder

1 tsp (5 g) vegan Sriracha sauce

Place the cornstarch in a small bowl. Stir with 2 tablespoons (30 ml) of water to dissolve. Place this slurry in a saucepan along with the remaining water, mirin, tamari, agave, ginger, shiitake powder and Sriracha. Whisk to combine.

Bring to a low boil, whisking constantly. Lower the heat to medium, and cook until thickened, about 10 minutes. Stir occasionally and adjust the heat as needed. Set aside.

PICKLED GINGER

Gluten-Free • In A Hurry • Oil-Free • Soy-Free

Store-bought pickled ginger often contains off-putting ingredients, so I wanted a homemade version with a short list of ingredients.

YIELD: ½ pint (237 ml)

3½ oz (100 g) fresh ginger root, peeled and thinly sliced

1½ tsp (4 g) coarse kosher salt

½ cup (120 ml) rice wine vinegar

2 tbsp (24 g) evaporated cane juice or organic granulated sugar

Place the ginger in a heat-safe, ½-pint (237-ml) canning jar. Place the salt, vinegar and sugar in a small saucepan. Bring to a boil, lower the heat to medium and cook until the sugar crystals are dissolved, about 2 minutes. Turn off the heat and let cool slightly. Carefully pour the brine on top of the ginger slices. Tighten the lid and let cool completely. Store in the refrigerator for at least 48 hours before use. Enjoy within 2 weeks.

PEPPERS IN A PICKLE

Gluten-Free • Oil-Free • Soy-Free

Pickles are my favorite condiment. What better way to add a flavor boost to the stuff you eat? The peppers pack quite a punch, so adjust according to your needs. You can always skip a few hot peppers and use equivalent amounts of extra bell pepper. Add them to your favorite sandwiches, Caramelized Jackfruit Tacos (page 20), Piri Piri Pit-za (page 73) or Summer Plate with Pickled Pepper Cream (page 106).

YIELD: 1 pint (473 ml)

---

1 cup (235 ml) distilled white vinegar

½ cup (100 g) evaporated cane juice or organic granulated sugar

2 tsp (6 g) coarse kosher salt

½ tsp mustard seeds

2 habaneros for spicy pickles, trimmed and sliced thinly (use 1 habanero and 1 bell pepper for milder pickles)

1 red Fresno pepper, trimmed and sliced thinly

¼ yellow bell pepper, sliced thinly

1 bird's eye chile (optional), trimmed and sliced thinly

¼ small red onion, chopped into bite-sized pieces, or to taste

2 small scallions, chopped

2 cloves garlic, peeled and gently smashed

3 tiny ribs celery from the yellow part of the heart

Place the vinegar, sugar and salt in a small saucepan. Bring to a boil, lower the heat to medium and cook until the sugar crystals are dissolved, about 2 minutes. Turn off the heat and let cool slightly.

Place the mustard seeds, peppers, chile (if using), onion, scallions, garlic and celery in a heat-safe, pint-sized canning jar. Carefully pour the brine on top. Tighten the lid and let cool completely. Store in the refrigerator for at least 48 hours before use. Enjoy within 2 weeks.

SPICY CITRUS SAUCE

Gluten-Free • Oil-Free • Soy-Free

This is a zingy, bright sauce that's just perfect with burritos (page 70), chili (page 116) and salad dressings (page 119). Be sure to use freshly squeezed orange juice because even the "not made from concentrate" kind bought at the store will yield disappointing results.

YIELD: Scant 1 cup (220 ml)

2⅔ cups (630 ml) fresh orange juice

2 tsp (10 ml) lime juice

1 tbsp (20 g) agave nectar

¼–½ tsp chipotle powder, to taste

½ tsp toasted cumin seeds

2 minced cloves garlic

¼ cup plus 2 tbsp (60 g) minced red onion

Scant ½ tsp smoked sea salt

Combine the orange juice, lime juice, agave, chipotle powder, cumin seeds, garlic, onion and salt in a medium saucepan. Bring to a boil, then reduce the heat to a low-bubbling simmer. Cook down until the sauce is reduced to ¼ of the original volume, with a thickness similar to compote. This will take about 1 hour. Be sure to stir frequently, and adjust the heat as needed.

Set aside to cool before transferring to an airtight jar. Store in the refrigerator for up to 2 weeks.

CHEATER GOCHUJANG PASTE

Gluten-Free

This spicy, deeply flavorful Korean paste is becoming easier to purchase from regular grocery stores these days. But it's always good to have a homemade alternative at hand. I use it in sausages (page 38), bowls (page 41), tacos (page 42) and more. I even love pairing a little bit of it with a crunchy nut butter for a savory, spicy PB&J version.

YIELD: 1 cup plus 1 tablespoon (340 g) paste

½ cup (144 g) white miso

½ cup (160 g) agave nectar

⅔ cup (160 ml) water

5 tbsp (40 g) gochugaru (Korean red chile powder)

1 tsp (2 g) onion powder

½ tsp garlic powder

¼ tsp coarse kosher salt

1 tsp (5 ml) brown rice vinegar

1 tsp (5 ml) toasted sesame oil

In a medium saucepan, whisk to combine the miso, agave, water, gochugaru, onion powder and garlic powder. On medium heat, heat the mixture until it starts to bubble slightly. Lower to a simmer and cook until it reaches the consistency of tomato paste, about 15 to 20 minutes. Be sure to stir frequently throughout the cooking process! Turn off the heat.

Whisk occasionally until the paste reaches room temperature, about 15 minutes to 1 hour depending on the season. Whisk the salt, vinegar and sesame oil into the paste. Transfer to an airtight container, and store in the refrigerator for up to 3 weeks.

*See photo on page 39.

MUSHROOM DASHI

Gluten-Free • In A Hurry • Oil-Free • Soy-Free

Mushroom dashi is the soaking liquid obtained from rehydrating dried shiitake mushrooms. It is used to bring extra umami to many dishes, such as Fish-Free Sauce (page 172), Chazuke (page 33) and many more. Use the rehydrated mushrooms anywhere you want, such as Kinoko Gohan (page 30), Tamarind Miso Soup (page 34), 'Fu-mami Broth and Veggies (page 13) or Asian-Inspired Fondue (page 19).

Choose high quality, preferably organic, dried shiitake mushrooms to prepare your dashi.

YIELD: 1½ cups (355 ml) mushroom dashi, 6 ounces (170 g) rehydrated mushrooms

---

1 oz (28 g) organic dried shiitake mushrooms

2 cups (470 ml) cold or room-temperature filtered water

For best results, choose the overnight version. The longer the soak, the more flavorful the dashi. Alternatively, the quick method is to use warm water and soak the mushrooms for 20 minutes until they are soft without being mushy.

Lightly brush your mushroom caps clean with a pastry brush or mushroom-cleaning brush. Place in a large bowl or a glass measuring cup (such as Pyrex), and cover with filtered water until fully submerged. Stir gently to make sure all the mushrooms will be hydrated. Cover with a lid or plastic wrap, and store in the refrigerator overnight.

The next day, line a fine-mesh sieve with a paper towel to catch impurities. Place the sieve on top of a bowl or glass measuring cup. Gently squeeze the mushrooms over the dashi container to get extra liquid out. Store the dashi in an airtight container in the refrigerator for up to 3 days.

Store the rehydrated mushrooms in an airtight container in the refrigerator for up to 2 days.

*See photo on page 183.

KOMBU DASHI

Gluten-Free • In A Hurry • Oil-Free • Soy-Free

This is a seaweed-based equivalent to umami-rich Mushroom Dashi (page 181). You can use either dashi interchangeably depending on your preference and combine them as well.

YIELD: 4 cups (940 ml) kombu dashi

0.4-oz (10-g) piece of dried kombu (kelp) (about 1 4-inch [10-cm] square)

4 cups (940 ml) cold or room-temperature filtered water

Gently wipe the kombu clean with a damp cloth. Use a clean pair of scissors to make a couple of 1-inch (2.5-cm) slits in the kombu. This step helps promote the extraction of flavor. Place the kombu in a large, sealable mason jar or bottle. Pour the filtered water on top, and seal closed. Let the kombu soak overnight in the refrigerator.

Alternatively, if you prefer a boiling method, soak the kombu in filtered water overnight. Transfer to a medium pot, and heat on medium heat. Just before the water comes to a full boil, remove the kombu and follow the next steps.

For either method, line a fine-mesh sieve with a paper towel to catch impurities. Place the sieve on top of a bowl or glass measuring cup as the recipient for the dashi. Remove and discard the kombu. Store the resulting dashi in the refrigerator for up to 3 days.

RED CURRY PASTE

Gluten-Free • Oil-Free

Store-bought red curry pastes vary wildly in flavor and can even contain fish sauce. So your best bet really is to go with delicious homemade paste. But if you have a good favorite vegan brand already, then by all means use it instead. Be sure to check that it doesn't contain shrimp paste! If they're easier to find, you can replace the Japanese red dried chile peppers with the same amount of bird's eye chiles. Kaffir lime leaves can also be difficult to locate. Substituting lime juice will be undoubtedly less authentic, but it will still yield a tasty result. Note that the color of the outcome might be browner than pictured depending on the peppers used.

YIELD: ½ cup (135 g) packed paste

---

12 Japanese red dried chile peppers, cored and seeded

1½ cups (355 ml) hot water

2¼ tsp (5 g) coriander seeds, toasted

¼ tsp whole white peppercorn

6 fresh red Thai chiles, trimmed and seeded if desired (depends on your heat tolerance)

¼ cup (40 g) minced shallot

1¾ tbsp (15 g) minced garlic

3 scant tbsp (12 g) minced fresh lemongrass

1 tbsp (6 g) minced fresh galangal or ginger root

1 fresh Kaffir lime leaf, finely minced (Substitute 1 tbsp [15 ml] fresh lime juice)

1½ tbsp (12 g) fresh cilantro stems

1½ tsp (8 ml) reduced-sodium tamari

½ tsp coarse kosher salt

Place the dried peppers in a heat-proof bowl and add hot water on top. Soak until softened, about 40 minutes. Drain the pepper and reserve the soaking liquid for other uses. You can store the liquid in an airtight jar in the refrigerator for up to 1 week.

Use a larger mortar and pestle to prepare your paste, or use a small food processor. Note that the mortar and pestle will require quite a bit of elbow grease. Start by finely grinding the coriander seeds and peppercorn. Combine in a separate bowl with the rest of the ingredients and pound in several small batches. This might take up to 20 minutes, and you deserve a cookie when you're done.

Alternatively, place the coriander seeds and peppercorn in a spice grinder. Grind to a fine powder. Place the coriander-pepper mixture, Thai chiles, shallot, garlic, lemongrass, galangal, lime leaves, cilantro, tamari and salt in a small food processor and process until blended and relatively smooth. Add chile-soaking water, 1 tablespoon (15 ml) at a time, if the mixture has trouble moving around. Stop the machine occasionally to scrape the paste from the sides of the bowl with a rubber spatula.

Store in the refrigerator in an airtight container for up to 2 weeks. Or freeze in individual portions in an ice cube tray reserved for foods that potentially stain; they will keep for up to 2 months.

POMEGRANATE MOLASSES

Gluten-Free • Oil-Free • Soy-Free

This molasses is sweet, tangy and so perfect you'll want to drizzle the stuff over everything! You should be able to find pomegranate molasses at the store, but it's such a breeze to make at home and the results are even better to boot.

YIELD: 1 cup (235 ml)

4 cups (940 ml) unsweetened pomegranate juice

3 tbsp (45 ml) lemon juice

3 tbsp (60 g) agave nectar

Place the pomegranate juice, lemon juice and agave in a saucepan. Bring to a low boil, stirring frequently. Lower the heat and simmer on medium-low until the liquid is thickened and reduced to a quarter of the original amount, about 1 cup (235 ml). This will take approximately 1 hour.

Keep an eye on the molasses as it cooks, adjusting the temperature if necessary, and stir frequently to prevent scorching. The risk of scorching becomes higher the more the molasses cooks down.

Let it cool to room temperature before transferring to a glass container. Don't transfer immediately as the high heat of the molasses could break the glass. Once cooled, cover with a tight-fitting lid and store in the refrigerator for up to 1 month.

JAPANESE CARROT PICKLES

Gluten-Free • In A Hurry • Soy-Free

While these carrot pickles taste great on their own, their flavor and texture truly shine when paired with other components, such as in the Chazuke (page 33), Indonesian-Inspired Rice Pancakes (page 105), 'Fu-mami Broth and Veggies (page 13) or simply served alongside Asian-Inspired Fondue (page 19).

YIELD: 1 (25-ounce [750-ml]) jar

---

4 large carrots, peeled and trimmed, cut into 2-inch (5-cm) chunks, thinly sliced lengthwise with a mandoline slicer

½ cup (120 ml) brown rice vinegar or unseasoned rice vinegar

2 tbsp (30 ml) mirin

1 tbsp (7 g) black sesame seeds

1½ tsp (8 ml) toasted sesame oil

1 tsp (5 ml) ume plum vinegar

1½ tsp (5 g) coarse kosher salt

1 clove garlic, grated

Place the carrots in a medium pot of boiling water and blanch 15 seconds. Drain well. Whisk the vinegar, mirin, sesame seeds, sesame oil, vinegar, salt and garlic in a medium bowl.

Gently fold the carrots into the mixture. Transfer to a large canning jar and close the lid tightly. Store in the refrigerator for at least 24 hours before use, and use within 2 weeks.

SAVORY SWEET FINISHING SAUCE

Gluten-Free

This well-balanced, subtly spiced finishing sauce hits all the right notes! Use it in the Caramelized Jackfruit Tacos (page 20), or try it as a dipping or glazing sauce for Asian-inspired dishes. For best results, look for fermented black beans that only contain beans and salt.

YIELD: 2 cups (545 g) sauce

---

1 cup (210 g) fresh pineapple chunks, minced

1/2 cup plus 1 1/2 tsp (128 ml) water, divided, for cornstarch slurry

1/2 cup (120 ml) rice wine vinegar

1/4 cup (55 g) packed organic light brown sugar

1/4 cup (40 g) fermented black beans, rinsed

1/4 cup (80 g) agave nectar

1/4 cup (60 ml) reduced-sodium tamari

1/4 cup (40 g) minced red or white onion

1 small serrano pepper or 1 bird's eye chile, cored, seeded and minced

2 tsp (5 g) roasted sesame seeds

2 tsp (6 g) minced garlic

1 tsp (5 ml) toasted sesame oil

1/2 tsp coarse kosher salt

1/4 tsp ground ginger

1/4 tsp Chinese Five-Spice Powder (page 162) or store-bought

1 1/2 tsp (4 g) organic cornstarch

In a medium saucepan, place the pineapple, 1/2 cup (120 ml) of water, vinegar, sugar, black beans, agave, tamari, onion, serrano pepper, sesame seeds, garlic, sesame oil, salt, ginger and five-spice powder. Bring to a boil, then lower the heat and simmer at a low boil for 20 minutes. Stir occasionally and adjust the heat as needed. Blend the mixture using an immersion blender or regular blender and set aside.

Place the cornstarch in a small bowl. Add 1 1/2 teaspoons (8 ml) of water to the cornstarch and stir to dissolve. Place the saucepan back onto the stove. Stir the cornstarch slurry into the mixture. Heat on medium heat, and cook until thickened to the consistency of barbecue sauce, about 10 minutes. Use a whisk to stir occasionally and adjust the heat as needed. Store the cooled sauce in an airtight container in the refrigerator for up to 2 weeks.

Use as a finishing sauce for vegan protein (seitan, tofu or tempeh) and veggies. Add the desired amount of sauce during the last 2 to 3 minutes of cooking until absorbed and slightly caramelized. Be mindful of the splatters when the sauce hits the hot pan; use caution and cover with a splatter screen or a lid to prevent messiness.

ASIAN PEAR PICKLES

Gluten-Free • In A Hurry • Oil-Free • Soy-Free

Despite what the instructions below say, I plead guilty to not peeling the Asian pears (aka nashi fruit). It works well if you buy organic fruit and you eat the pickles quickly—they won't have time to muck up the brine. I can eat the whole jar in one shot so that's never been an issue. It's highly likely you won't show control either, which is fine because they're great for snacking. Just be sure to keep enough for the Pulled Jackfruit Rolls (page 10).

FYI: The flavor of the tea is quite subtle and pairs so well with the sweetness of the fruit.

YIELD: 1 (25-ounce [750 ml]) jar

---

3 tbsp (45 ml) lemon juice

1-inch (2.5-cm) knob fresh ginger root, peeled and grated

5 small fresh Asian pears (about 1 pound [500 g]), peeled, quartered, cored and thinly sliced

1 tsp (3 g) coarse kosher salt

$\frac{1}{2}$ cup (100 g) evaporated cane juice or organic granulated sugar

1 cup (235 ml) rice wine vinegar

1 teabag (1$\frac{1}{2}$ tsp [3 g]) Lapsang Souchong tea

Place the lemon juice and ginger in a large bowl. As you slice the pears (using a mandoline slicer if available), gently fold them into the lemon juice to prevent browning. Set aside.

Place the salt, sugar and vinegar in a small saucepan. Bring to a boil, lower the heat and cook until the sugar crystals are dissolved, about 1 to 2 minutes. Remove from the heat and add the teabag. Steep for 10 minutes. Gently squeeze the teabag and discard. Pour the brine on top of the pear slices. Don't be concerned if the pears aren't fully covered at first; the liquid will soften them after a few minutes.

Transfer to a large canning jar and close the lid tightly. Store in the refrigerator for at least 2 hours before use, and use within 2 weeks.

PINEAPPLE (OR MANGO!) PEPPER JELLY

Gluten-Free • Oil-Free • Soy-Free

Most of the pepper jelly recipes I see make use of some pectin powder, but I wanted to use actual fruit to play that thickening role. My favorite way to use pepper jelly is in nut or seed butter sandwiches. You could also serve a little with basic scrambled tofu or in other sandwiches. Or even use the jelly in quesadillas made with your favorite vegan cheese! Or, better yet, try it on Crunchy Corn Waffles (page 74).

If you decide to make a large batch of the jelly for canning and find all that chopping action daunting, pulse the veggies in a food processor to mince them and save some time.

YIELD: 1 cup (310 g) jelly

---

1 cup (210 g) minced fresh pineapple or mango

1 hot pepper of choice, cored, seeded and minced (I love habanero peppers in this)

1 small bell pepper (any color), cored, seeded and minced

$\frac{1}{2}$ cup (120 ml) distilled white vinegar

Juice from $\frac{1}{2}$ of a lime (1 tbsp [15 ml])

$\frac{1}{2}$ cup (160 g) brown rice syrup

$\frac{1}{4}$ cup (80 g) agave nectar

$\frac{1}{4}$ tsp coarse kosher salt

Combine the pineapple, peppers, vinegar, lime juice, brown rice syrup, agave and salt in a medium saucepan. Bring to a slow boil on medium-high heat, then lower the heat so that the mixture doesn't bubble over. Stir frequently and simmer until quite thick, glossy and reduced to about half the original amount. This will take at least 1 hour. Keep in mind the jelly will continue to thicken as it cools.

If you don't plan on canning the jelly, let it cool to room temperature before transferring to an airtight jar. Store in the refrigerator for up to 2 weeks. If you want to can it for gifting or later use, ladle the hot jelly into a sterilized mason jar and process in a hot water bath for 5 minutes.

MEET AND GREET YOUR NEW BFFS (BOLD-FLAVORED FRIENDS)

A NOTE ON KITCHEN TOOLS

The good news is you don't need a whole bunch of fancy kitchen tools to work with this book. I don't use a dehydrator, nor am I the proud owner of a high-speed blender. Shocking, I know. While these tools do come in handy and yield amazing results if you already have them, I know I'm not the only one who simply doesn't have the budget or counter space for more kitchen equipment.

I use an immersion blender for most blending work, but a counter blender will be perfect if that's what you have handy. When the going gets a little tougher or when vegetables need to be chopped, a medium-sized, regular food processor takes care of the rest.

I also occasionally work with a mandoline slicer to thinly slice vegetables, but using a well-sharpened chef's knife on a sturdy and steady cutting board instead will do the trick. A quick, friendly reminder that if you use a mandoline slicer, be sure to protect your fingers and knuckles! Not that I speak from experience or anything. (Ow!)

And finally, if you have a few good pots and pans of various sizes, then you're ready to get started. Now that was relatively painless, wasn't it?

SUREFIRE WAYS TO BRING BOLD FLAVORS TO YOUR VEGAN TABLE

Everyone deserves bold flavors on their plates! There are many ways to refuse blandness in your vegan food, without having to stick solely to the most obvious choices, such as salt and pepper. Add peppy and zesty ingredients that imbue life into dishes. Or choose umami (page 199) to bring bold flavors. Try cooking techniques that make use of flavor-packed fermented or caramelized foods. The important thing to remember is that the goal of bringing boldness onto your plate is to enhance the natural flavors of the food, not cover them up.

If you've already met your perfect match in the way of store-bought sauces and more, know that those shortcuts are absolutely okay. While I have a fondness for all things homemade, I also give a major thumbs-up to anything that cuts down on preparation time, especially when you are in a rush. What I love about using homemade foods, such as curry and harissa pastes, finishing sauces and more, is that you control what goes into them. You also get to decide how strong the flavors will be. Clearly, everyone has a different tolerance for heat levels or sodium levels. Using just the right amount of every single ingredient makes the time it takes to prepare these staples at home entirely worthwhile. Be the master of your own boldness!

An invaluable health benefit of splurging on natural bold-flavored ingredients is that the addition of extra salt won't be as necessary. Take the case of Shichimi Togarashi (page 161): You'd be hard-pressed to guess there isn't a flake of salt to be found in this Japanese spice mixture. Sprinkle it over your meal (pages 19 and 33), or coat cashew cheese (page 123) with it, and you'll see it delivers a generous palette of flavors while being entirely sodium-free.

When I moved to the United States from Switzerland, I'll admit I was a bit of a wimp when it came to spiciness in food. After years of living in California and being exposed to fantastic Mexican food, my taste buds are now made of steel. Rest assured that I've kept in mind that not everyone wants their mouth ablaze. My recipes keep the heat levels moderate for the most part, and I offer alternatives for even milder options.

If your tolerance is on the low side, always remove the seeds from your fresh peppers: This is where most of the heat resides. Oh, and be sure to wear kitchen gloves as you do this, because something on your face is bound to start itching right after you've cored the hot peppers (Murphy's Law #28492895), and the pain can be blinding.

Whenever available and affordable, and if you are so inclined, try to purchase organic ingredients.

VEGAN SOURCES OF BOLD FLAVOR

Caramelization: Roast, sear or grill fruit and vegetables to bring out their sweetness. Try the Caramelized Jackfruit Tacos (page 20) or the Peachy Tamari Creamy Farina (page 126).

Citrus: Add the zest, juice or extract from orange, lemon or lime. Try the Orange Marmite Noodle Bowl (page 49) or the Red Curry Scramble with Lime-y Broccoli (page 98).

Dried hot peppers: Rehydrate whole peppers (page 185) or use them in the form of flakes or powder. Try the Tahini Harissa Toast with Gomashio (page 109) or the Red Curry Paste (page 185).

Fermented foods: Incorporate fermented black beans, kimchi (page 27) or miso into your dishes. Try the Savory Sweet Finishing Sauce (page 190) or the Asian-Inspired Fondue (page 19).

Fresh hot peppers: Use a little or a lot of jalapeño, Thai or serrano peppers for a moderate to mega kick in the taste buds. Try the Peppers in a Pickle (page 176) or the Very Tahini Teffballs and Dressing (page 81).

Nuts and seeds: Toast them slowly in a skillet or moderate oven to release their buttery flavor. Try the Savory Asian-Flavored Granola (page 64) or the Soy Pomegranate-Glazed Baby Eggplants with Dukkah (page 55).

Pickled fruits and vegetables: Create extra dimension by utilizing pickles! Try the Pulled Jackfruit Rolls (page 10) or the Piri Piri Pit-za (page 73).

Pomegranate Molasses (page 186): Drizzle on top of savory and sweet recipes for tasty tartness. Try the Red Chana Dal Mujaddara (page 77) or Pomegranate Strawberry Granita (page 149).

Spices: Add coriander, Ras el Hanout (page 159), turmeric, sumac and other spice combinations to jazz up your meals. Try the Harira (page 102) or the Roasted Cabbage Slices with Chermoula and Chickpeas (page 92).

Sauces and pastes: Maximize greatness by coating your food with even more flavor. Try the Fish-Free Sauce (page 172) or the Harissa Paste (page 165).

Umami-rich vegan ingredients: Meet the fifth taste on page 199. Then try the 'Fu-mami Broth and Veggies (page 13) or the Homemade Kimchi (page 27).

A NOTE ON UMAMI

There are five basic tastes people can experience as they eat and drink: sweet, sour, bitter, salty and umami. Umami is known as the fifth taste. The word is a neologism coined from the Japanese word umai, which literally translates to "delicious taste." However, in this instance it isn't used to describe deliciousness; instead, it is a signal for the savory taste we experience from the foods we eat.

I bet you are more than familiar with the experience of dipping salty, crispy french fries in savory-sweet ketchup. Think about the resulting taste explosion in your mouth. Are you salivating yet? That's umami for you.

Umami was discovered and named over a century ago by professor Kikunae Ikeda, a scientist who worked at Tokyo Imperial University, now known as the University of Tokyo.

The three components of umami are:

Glutamate: an amino acid, also known as the building protein in the body. It's the main component of umami, and it's naturally present in food proteins, such as kombu, fresh mushrooms, broccoli and onions. As far as non-vegan foods go, glutamate is also found in cheese. Professor Kikunae Ikeda identified glutamate in 1908 when he extracted it from seaweed broth and determined it was the source of the broth's savory taste. A frequent question is whether glutamate contains gluten due to their similar names. It does not.

Inosinate: a nucleotide, also known as the building block of DNA or RNA. It's found in animal-based foods and, therefore, clearly won't be used in this book. Inosinate was identified by Shintaro Kodama in 1913.

Guanylate: another nucleotide. It's found in dried mushrooms, such as shiitake mushrooms, and in cooked potatoes. This nucleotide was identified by Akira Kuninaka in 1957.

In 2000, a team of scientists at the University of Miami discovered that human tongues have special taste receptors for umami. That's a major step forward, considering receptors for both sweet and bitter tastes have yet to be recognized.

While umami is highly prevalent in protein-rich, animal-based foods, it's thankfully easy to re-create this experience in vegan cooking by layering umami-rich ingredients to match the results obtained in non-vegan cooking. Combining foods that contain glutamate with ingredients rich in guanylate means that you'll get the most well-rounded and palatable umami flavors.

Here are a couple of examples. Check out the Sweet Potato Fries dipped in Sriracha Ketchup on page 60. The sweet potatoes and ketchup have glutamate galore, and the fries are also dusted with powdered dried mushrooms (rich in guanylate) and just a little bit of salt.

Another example is the aptly named 'Fu-mami Broth and Veggies on page 13, brimming with beer, kimchi and its brine, smoky Lapsang Souchong tea, spicy gochujang paste and dried shiitake powder. It is the umami to end all umami.

UMAMI-RICH VEGAN INGREDIENTS

- ☐ Aged balsamic vinegar
- ☐ Fermented foods, such as vegan kimchi, miso, sauerkraut, tamari and tempeh
- ☐ Matcha green tea
- ☐ Mushrooms, such as fresh or dried shiitake and porcini
- ☐ Nutritional yeast
- ☐ Olives
- ☐ Potatoes and sweet potatoes
- ☐ Seaweed, such as kombu, nori and wakame
- ☐ Tomatoes, including tomato paste, sun-dried tomatoes and ketchup
- ☐ Ume plum vinegar
- ☐ Vegan beer and wine
- ☐ Vegan Worcestershire sauce
- ☐ Yeast extract, such as Marmite, Vegemite and Cenovis

A NOTE ON MSG

Monosodium glutamate (MSG) has been a controversial subject for years. Glutamate can be found naturally in the foods already mentioned here, but MSG is synthetically grown and far more concentrated in glutamates. This high concentration has been claimed to trigger severe symptoms, such as headache and nausea, in groups of people who are highly sensitive to it. A small subset of people can also be sensitive to lower levels of glutamates, even those that are naturally occurring in food. These claims have been frequently disputed and doubted, especially when studies were performed and no reactions were triggered. However, many of us choose to steer clear of foods that contain added MSG.

It should be noted that the U.S. Food and Drug Administration (FDA) deems the addition of MSG in food as being "generally recognized as safe" (GRAS). Thankfully, MSG and other glutamate-rich ingredients must be clearly identified on food labels. You'll find them listed as monosodium glutamate, autolyzed yeast and hydrolyzed protein. We can all use our discretion and choose to consume or avoid MSG. As always, knowledge is power, and you alone can make the right choices for you and your family.

KNOW YOUR OTHER INGREDIENTS

I live in a growing town where it's slowly getting easier to find vegan ingredients at regular grocery stores or international food stores. Yet there are still times when I need to order items online. Oftentimes I am looking for lower prices because everyone loves a bargain.

While I try to avoid using harder-to-find ingredients, here is a list of things you might need more information about and a few that you might have to order online or special order at your favorite store.

Aleppo pepper flakes: Popular in Middle Eastern and Mediterranean cuisines, these crushed pepper flakes are slightly smoky, fruity and milder than regular red pepper flakes. They can be found at international food markets or online.

Dried shiitake powder: I purchase this organic powder in bulk. Use it in broth powder and to boost the umami flavor of virtually any dish. If unavailable, you can make your own by using a coffee grinder or small food processor to grind gently brushed dried shiitake mushrooms. While the powder might not be super fine, it's perfectly okay as the small pieces will rehydrate as they cook in liquids provided by the recipes. It's quite popular in the cooking world to enjoy raw powdered dried mushrooms (such as dried porcini) combined with other ingredients to season food, but I cannot recommend eating dried shiitake mushrooms in uncooked form because a small subset of people reportedly get a rash-like reaction to shiitake mushrooms when eaten raw.

Gochugaru: Also known as Korean red chile powder or Korean red pepper flakes. The consistency is closer to that of a coarse powder. Gochugaru is smokier and slightly milder than regular red pepper flakes, so I don't recommend subbing one for the other. Gochugaru can sometimes be found at international food markets, but your best bet might be to purchase it online. Note that the color of gochugaru may vary depending on the brand, going from redder to browner. Don't fret if your results look different than pictured in this book, as the flavor won't be affected. I've used various brands with equally tasty outcomes.

Gochujang sauce: This fermented sauce is made of gochugaru (Korean red chile powder), fermented soybeans, glutinous rice and salt. Its popularity is on the rise and is starting to match that of Sriracha sauce. It is fairly easy to find at regular markets these days. If you're looking for an absolutely delicious—albeit inauthentic—option, try the Cheater Gochujang Paste recipe (page 180).

Kimchi: Behold, the almighty Korean fermented Napa cabbage! Pepped up with gochugaru, this ingredient is put to good use in quite a few recipes in this book. You can find great versions at most grocery stores. Just be sure to check the ingredients list, as not all of them are vegan: Fish sauce is a commonly added ingredient. Spice levels also vary, so choose the one that best suits your heat tolerance. Or, better yet, make your own (page 27).

Lapsang Souchong: A black tea with a lovely, deeply smoky flavor, originating from China. Lapsang Souchong can be found at most well-stocked tea stores or online. The brand I use is akin to a powder, and it contains $1\frac{1}{2}$ teaspoons (3 g) of tea per bag.

Matcha green tea powder: While this antioxidant-rich, jewel-green tea is most frequently used as a frothy hot beverage, using it in both savory and sweet applications will also showcase its beautiful umami depth. Be sure to purchase culinary-grade matcha for cooking, rather than the costlier premium-grade version.

Miso: This Japanese fermented soybean paste is full of flavor and umami! Red miso (akamiso) is the one that holds the most umami power. It is also much more strongly flavored than another favorite, white miso (shiromiso), which is sweeter-tasting and has a lighter umami potency. The flavor and strength of miso varies with the brand, so you might have to shop around until you find the perfect match for your taste. I highly recommend purchasing organic miso. If you are avoiding soy, there is some delicious chickpea miso available on the market but it can be a little trickier to locate depending on where you live.

Nutritional yeast: More popular than ever, even in non-vegan circles, this cheesy-tasting deactivated yeast brings umami and depth to many dishes. I purchase the kind that is supplemented with vitamin B_{12}, from the Red Star brand. You can get a large quantity for a fair price at Bulkfoods.com if you live in the United States. Note that the measuring weight of nutritional yeast has been found to vary depending on the brand. The weight can even vary based on whether it is stored at room temperature, in the refrigerator, or in the freezer.

Plant-based milks: With the wide variety of plant-based milks available today, either in the refrigerated section or in shelf-stable form, you really just have to take your pick. If you haven't found your favorite yet, try a few until you find the creaminess and flavor you love the most. My current go-to is cashew milk. I recommend purchasing unsweetened plain plant-based milks because those are the most versatile for both savory and sweet applications.

Pomegranate molasses: Tart and sweet, pomegranate molasses is perfect to use drizzled on both savory and sweet dishes. This Middle Eastern treat is made by cooking down pomegranate juice to a syrup-like state. You can find a super easy recipe on page 186, or you can purchase a bottle at international food markets or online.

Sambal oelek: A spicy Asian sauce made of red chile, vinegar and salt. A little goes a long way as it is quite fiery. On a personal note, I grew up dipping summer rolls in this sauce and my love for it may well be even more endless than my love for Sriracha sauce.

Sumac: This tart and lemony ground-up berry is used in savory Middle Eastern dishes, and it is a great addition to sweets as well. It can be found at international food markets and online.

Tamari: Tamari is a Japanese-style, deeply flavored soy sauce. Unlike regular soy sauce, it's gluten-free. Choose organic, reduced-sodium tamari if available because it's easier to add extra salt than it is to correct a dish that's too salty. If you cannot find tamari, go with reduced-sodium soy sauce but keep in mind that the gluten-free recipe icon won't stand in recipes where this substitution is made.

Tamarind paste or concentrate: Tamarind is a sticky and sour paste made from the flesh of tamarind fruit. It can be used in chutneys and curries, and it's also brilliant in Tamarind Miso Soup (page 34) and Quick and Easy Pad Thai (page 37). Tamarind paste can be found at international food markets or online.

Tempeh: Some people find this fermented soybean cake has a bitter flavor when used straight out of the package. It seems to depend on the brand used. To solve this potential issue, tempeh can be steamed before use. Place the tempeh block or slices in a saucepan. Cover with water and bring to a boil. Reduce the heat, cover with a lid and simmer for 10 minutes. Drain well before use. Note that hot, steamed tempeh will absorb marinades faster than tempeh used straight from the refrigerator.

Tofu: I prefer using super firm tofu rather than extra-firm tofu because it means no pressing is required. Extra-firm tofu shouldn't be confused with silken tofu, which only needs to be drained but not pressed. If you only find extra-firm tofu, be sure to press it to remove most of the unwanted water it contains and to obtain firmer results. Place several layers of clean paper towels on a plate. Drain the water from the package of tofu. Place the tofu on the paper towels and top with more paper towels. Place a heavy cutting board, books or a can on top to weigh it down. Drain every half hour until very little liquid remains. To avoid wasting paper towels, consider purchasing a tofu press, which is specifically designed for that use. For even firmer results, freeze the package of extra-firm tofu, then thaw it out and proceed as described above.

Ume plum vinegar: Also known as umeboshi vinegar, this salty and sour concoction is the umami-rich by-product of the umeboshi plum pickling process. A little goes a long way, so a bottle should last you for quite some time.

Urfa pepper flakes: Also known as Isot pepper or Isot biber. (Biber is the Turkish word for pepper.) These mildly spicy, smoky, crushed pepper flakes are used in the same way as Aleppo pepper flakes. The Turkish chile pepper has undertones of raisin, chocolate and even tobacco. It can be ordered online or found at some international food markets.

Yeast extract: A sticky, salty, strongly flavored food spread. A little goes a long way, so don't be too generous when adding a layer to your vegan buttered toast! The most popular brands are Marmite (U.K.), Vegemite (Australia) and Cenovis (Switzerland). These products contain autolyzed yeast extract, which is part of the MSG controversy (see page 200). Autolyzed yeast extract naturally contains a high amount of glutamates, but not in as high a concentration as MSG. Nevertheless, jars of yeast extract clearly label "autolyzed yeast extract" as being part of the ingredients so that anyone with allergies and food sensitivities can make an informed decision.

ACKNOWLEDGMENTS

My gratitude goes out to the Page Street Publishing team for welcoming me on my first solo cookbook adventure. Will Kiester, Marissa Giambelluca, Meg Baskis and Meg Palmer: You truly are the cat's meow. It's been a privilege to get to work with super talented copyeditor Jenna Patton again. Thank you so much for making this book the best it can be!

An endless supply of thank yous to the brilliant testers and friends who worked so hard to ensure my recipes were worthy of making it into this book: Courtney Blair, Michelle Cavigliano (myzoetrope.com), Shannon Davis, Susan Gottlieb, Rochelle Kregar, Monique and Michel Narbel-Gimzia, Jenna Patton (tastefulediting.com), Monika Soria Caruso and Liz Wyman.

To my family, for never failing to support me when I lose confidence and for cheering me on, always: Mamou, Papou and Chaz, you are irreplaceable and loved. Merci infiniment.

To Constanze (seitanismymotor.com) and Joni (justthefood.com), for their friendship through the years. Respect your elders!

Last but definitely not least, thank you for your support and for holding this book in your hands. I hope you enjoy cooking from it as much as I enjoyed writing it.

ABOUT THE AUTHOR

Celine Steen is the co-author of several vegan cookbooks, including *The Complete Guide to Vegan Food Substitutions, The Complete Guide to Even More Vegan Food Substitutions, Vegan Sandwiches Save the Day!* and many more.

Celine styled and photographed the food in all the cookbooks she co-wrote, as well as those of several other authors including Joni Marie Newman (*Vegan Food Gifts* and more), Natalie Slater (*Bake and Destroy: Good Food for Bad Vegans*) and Cara Reed (*Decadent Gluten-Free Vegan Baking*). Her food photographs have also been featured in several photography books and e-books.

Got questions or comments? Get in touch at hello@celinesteen.com.

You can also visit havecakewilltravel.com for updates and bonus recipes and follow @celinensteen on Instagram.

INDEX